THE **REALLY, REALLY, REALLY EASY**

STEP-BY-STEP GUIDE TO CREATING YOUR

FAMILY TREE

USING YOUR COMPUTER

for absolute beginners of all ages

Gavin Hoole and Cheryl Smith

Contents

Read this before you start

GENEALOGY IS A PLEASANT JOURNEY, NOT AN OVERNIGHT DASH

The wonderful thing about genealogy is that there is no real urgency; you can work at it according to your own time availability. This is one of the reasons why so many people find building their family tree such an appealing hobby. You can work at it and then take a break for a few days, weeks, months or even years, until you feel the urge to pick up again where you left off.

THE JOURNEY IS FUN, BUT IT CAN HAVE SOME SURPRISES

You'll find that building a family tree can be a lot of fun as you discover new things about your ancestors. You'll be playing the role of a detective, a sleuth and a puzzle solver as you put together bits of information from different sources to build a picture of your family history and your roots.

Part of the fun will be negotiating your way through your ancestral mazes; and you'll discover some interesting things you didn't know about your ancestors.

- You will likely hit roadblocks and become frustrated. This book will show you how to minimize that likelihood.
- You'll discover conflicting information, so don't ever assume anything is correct until it's been verified by you.
- You will hear unexpected tales. Ancestors often had secrets: don't be too surprised if you discover that your grandfather's uncle was really his brother. During times of difficulty, such as the war years, newborn children of poor families were often passed off to a relative to raise, and a family secret was born.
- You may well find skeletons in your ancestral closets: adoptions and children born to unmarried parents were common but always kept a big secret. These secrets are only now being discovered as we go through our parents' and grandparents' personal belongings after their deaths. The first clue could be as simple as seeing that little girl in a family photograph and having no idea who she is and whether she is a relative or a just a friend.

The Internet is really a great benefit to genealogists, yet its vast database can sometimes be seen as quite overwhelming at first, particularly if one doesn't have the proper guidance. This book will give you that guidance.

 WORK YOUR WAY THROUGH EACH CHAPTER IN SEQUENCE This step-by-step workbook is designed to be used chapter by chapter. Working through it in its proper sequence will help you do 'first things first' and learn the correct ways of tackling the various genealogy processes and methodologies that follow in each subsequent chapter.

A COMPUTER IS A KEY TOOL IN GENEALOGY

This book assumes that you will have easy access to a computer with an Internet connection. These days, much of the information needed for developing one's family tree and family history is now available on the Internet. It is therefore almost essential to make use of this modern technology for the convenience and time savings it offers.

 MICROSOFT WINDOWS HAS BEEN USED FOR THIS BOOK The genealogy computer software covered in this book uses the Microsoft Windows operating system. If you are using some other operating system you will need to make adaptations accordingly when you work through those sections that include step-by-step procedures involving the genealogy software.

THE USER-FRIENDLY VISUAL SYSTEM

The same user-friendly visual system as used in all the books in this series makes it really, really, really easy for you to enjoy developing your own family tree.

Colour-coded text windows are used throughout the book so that you can see at a glance the type of information you're looking at:

- introductions and explanations in normal black text on a white background;

- step-by-step action procedures in yellow boxes;

- hints and tips in blue boxes;

- very important notes and warnings in boxes with red borders;

- supportive explanatory information in grey panels.

Where necessary, the detailed procedures are supported by illustrations to make learning easier.

TIP: THIS BOOK HAS A COMPANION WEBSITE

At our genealogy website you can download free genealogy software as well as forms and charts that you can use as you collect your ancestral data. The site also has hyperlinks to a number of useful genealogy websites for finding information about one's ancestors. Our website address is:

http://www.reallyeasycomputerbooks.com

Let's have some fun!

1 Getting organized

GENEALOGY DEFINED

Genealogy – with the third syllable ('al') pronounced as 'ol' (jee-nee-**ol**-uh-jee) – is essentially the study of a person's or group's family history (*ancestry* or *lineage*). The findings are documented in a family tree in the form of a pedigree chart, which sets out graphically the lines of ascent from one generation going back in time to each earlier generation. A pedigree chart normally spans several generations into the past and often even extends over a few centuries.

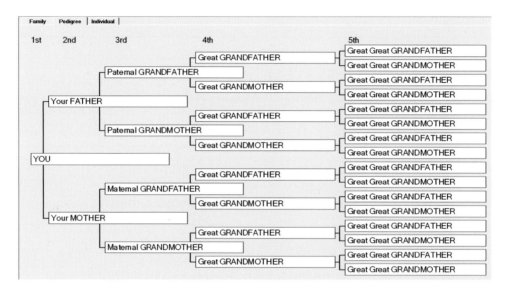

A 5-generation pedigree chart

A family history can also include interesting information, stories and biographies about a family's ancestors (where one's research findings make this possible). With the advent of computers, and the vast amount of information now available on the Internet, genealogy is emerging as one of the world's most popular hobbies.

Going back six generations in one family

Photos found in the family's basement archives at home. Left to right: (1) child with (2) mother, (3) grandmother, (4) great grandmother, (5) great great grandmother, (6) great great great grandmother

Until recent times exploring one's heritage could only be a very laborious task. It required lots of travelling to heritage sources – sometimes taking costly overseas trips – to delve into libraries and archives in order to track down the various generations of family members who came before us. Although this kind of work is still absolutely necessary to get accurate heritage information, nowadays the Internet provides an excellent and vast additional source of genealogical data and information.

These Internet databases can be very useful in pointing the researcher in the right direction, and in providing missing data not discovered through conventional methods. This enormous Internet data resource is the result of government archives and other organizations making their records available in this easily accessible way. And it is also thanks to many private individuals who have gone before us and done much of the spadework and generously shared their findings via the Internet. In time, you too could join the groups of people sharing their family history findings with others via the Internet.

AN OVERVIEW OF THE GENEALOGY JOURNEY

Whatever one's motives might be for getting started with genealogy, creating one's own family tree involves several essential activities. Some of these key activities take place concurrently, while some are repeated in a cyclical way. The key activities, as covered in this book, are:

1. **Establishing your main objective and focus:** This is where you determine your own personal motivation for going on a genealogical journey in the first place – where you set your overall long-term objective. This helps you save time and avoid getting sidetracked along the way. There are many avenues open to explore, especially with the proliferation of Internet websites; staying focused on your objective and knowing where you're heading will save you much time in the long run.
   As you progress, however, some interesting aspects may emerge about your past, aspects that you were not aware of at the outset; these new insights may well inspire you to make a conscious decision to adjust your focus and your longer-term objective.

2. **Setting short-term goals and doing the research:** This involves deciding which branch of your family you want to focus on for the next part of your investigations, and specifying definite short-term goals you want to achieve for that stage of your research. For example, you may decide that your next thrust is to find out about your paternal grandparents – when and where they were born, where they lived, and so on. You then do your research in a methodical way in order to achieve that specific goal before moving on to your next goal, perhaps for a different branch of the family.
   Your research should start in your own home, with you and your immediate family, and then move to your parents and grandparents, if they are still alive. It later broadens out further as you delve back generation after generation, searching through public records. The research will entail looking through family documents and photographs, interviewing family members and perhaps close friends who knew deceased family members very well. It will also involve using the Internet to search for information on the World Wide Web, and accessing public archives from libraries, government, military and church records, and the like.

3. **Recording and organizing your findings:** As you obtain new details about your ancestors, you record your findings accurately, checking and verifying data as necessary, and (very importantly) recording the source of each piece of information you gather so that the reliability of the details in your family tree can be assessed or validated. In these days of digital technology this process is usually done by means of an easy-to-use genealogy computer program (software) to computerize one's ancestry details and generate family tree charts and other reports and lists. Using specialized software saves a lot of time and makes creating standard genealogy reports really easy. The software also makes it possible

to share your findings with other genealogists worldwide via the Internet and e-mail. In this way people can help one another obtain missing information, by exchanging ancestry details about common family branches being researched by both parties.

4. **Continuously expanding and updating the details:** As you move along, you'll continue to expand your database and family information, and possibly correct some of the details too – such as names, dates and places – as new, more reliable information shows that earlier findings were not as accurate as first assumed.

5. **Putting your family tree and family history to good use:** This is the culmination of your many, many hours of interesting detective work, where you start to make use of your charts and supporting information to fulfil your original intent – be it publishing a book about your family history and lineage, establishing a family website, documenting inherited illnesses running through the generations of your bloodline, or simply establishing a solid basis for future generations of enthusiastic descendants to build on and use to keep your family history alive.

This chapter covers the first of these processes: establishing your focus and longer-term objectives. It also guides you into acquiring the tools you'll need for getting started.

DETERMINE YOUR LONGER-TERM OBJECTIVE

There are various reasons why people get interested in tracing their family history and plotting a family tree that shows their ancestors through the past centuries; the motives differ from person to person. Knowing what your own motivation is will help you establish your own focus and stay on track to avoid a lot of wasted time and frustration down the genealogy path. A checklist of some common reasons why people research their ancestry is provided below. Use it to help you determine your own motives and family history objective.

---

1 Tick off the item(s) that ring true for you and think of any other reasons not included in the list.

2 Summarize your focus by writing it down as your genealogy objective.

3 Keep your written objective at hand as a reminder of what you want to achieve.

Checklist for objective setting

❑ To find out who one's ancestors were, where they lived, and so on.

❑ To create a family tree that tells one's children about their roots and where they came from.

❑ To establish some facts in order to prove one's rights to an inheritance.

❑ To trace any inherited medical condition contributing to a present family member's ill-health.

❑ To find and meet unknown, distant relatives – second cousins, and the like.

❑ To find out about certain ancestors who are said to have been quite famous in their day.

❑ To explore the different mixed-race bloodlines from where one comes.

❑ To trace one's roots back to ancestors who were slaves.

❑ As an adopted person, to trace one's biological parents and ancestry.

❑ To get to the bottom of some rumours about one's 'murky' ancestry.

❑ To have a book published about one's family history.

❑ To trace one's immigrant roots back to one's homeland.

❑ To find out what crimes one's convict ancestor committed to justify his being sent to a colony.

PLAN FOR INFORMATION EXPANSION As you work back in time, gathering information on each individual – generation by generation – the amount of information you'll gather will grow exponentially. At every generation, the two parents each have their own two parents too; so two multiplies to four. Those four expand to eight more, and the eight to sixteen, and so on. With this exponential growth, by the time you reach the tenth generation back you will have collected information on 1,024 individuals. So a good filing system becomes an essential tool for genealogy.

SET UP YOUR FILING SYSTEM

Set up a simple alphabetical filing system in a box or cabinet, one that can easily be expanded as your search for ancestry information progresses. The filing system should store such things as old documents, photographs, love-letters, postcards, newspaper clippings, wedding invitations, passports, and more, depending on what your searching uncovers.

1 First, create a set of labelled file folders (or dividers), one for each surname that you'll be tracing. (e.g. a folder for **HOOLE**, a folder for **SMITH**, etc.)

2 In each of these folders, set up labelled sub-folders (as and when they are needed) in which to store specific documents you have collected pertaining to your 'HOOLE' or 'SMITH' ancestors, e.g.
- Sub-folders labelled **HOOLE-Marriage Certificates** and **HOOLE-Photographs** go into the main HOOLE folder, and so on.
- Sub-folders labelled **SMITH-Death Certificates, SMITH-Correspondence** go into the main SMITH folder, and so on.

Contents of a main surname folder
- A completed family tree chart (also called a pedigree chart)
- A completed family group chart that shows more details about each family than a pedigree chart can accommodate

Contents of a sub-folder (examples)
- last will and testaments
- certificates of birth, baptism, bar mitzvah, marriage (and other religious or traditional ceremonies), death
- adoption records
- passports
- photographs
- certificates and awards
- land deeds
- correspondence
- passenger lists
- military records
- newspaper articles, etc.
- anything else of relevance and interest that you come across that pertains to that family group

GATHER YOUR TOOLS OF THE TRADE

You'll soon be gathering your first lot of information to develop your family tree. We suggest that, before you get started with your research, you take some time now to gather the various items you'll need. Some of them you may already have at home; others you'll need to buy or download from the Internet. Use the following checklist to mark off each item once you have it.

Checklist of things you'll need to find or buy

❑ File folders – for storing photos and papers, as already explained

❑ Filing cabinet or storage boxes – for housing your folders and sub-folders of papers

❑ A 'treasure chest' – some kind of case or box for keeping non-paper memorabilia safely

❑ Briefcase or similar – for travelling with your documents, when you do field research

❑ Index cards – for quick cross-referencing where you've filed various items

❑ Acid-free folders – for safely protecting all your collected papers and photos

❑ Acid-free sheet protectors – for protecting original documents and photographs

❑ White cotton gloves – for handling any original old photographs and documents and preventing premature deterioration

Checklist of free computer files to download

❑ Pedigree Chart

❑ Family Group Record form

❑ Research Calendar

❑ Interview Record

❑ Interview Questionnaire Checklist

❑ Correspondence Record

❑ Source Summary form

❑ Genealogy computer software (Personal Ancestry File – 'PAF') – essential

❑ Installing PAF – installation instructions document

❑ Adobe Reader – if you don't already have it installed for reading PDF files

DOWNLOAD THE ESSENTIAL TOOLS

1 Connect to the Internet, and in your Web browser (e.g. Internet Explorer) type the following website address: **http://www.reallyeasycomputerbooks.com** and press ⌨Enter to go to our website.

2 Once there, on our Home Page click on **Enter Really Easy Computer Books Website** to open the first page.

3 Click on **Genealogy** to go to the genealogy section of the site.

4 At the Genealogy page, click on the **Downloads** link to access the list of free forms, charts and software that you can download to your computer. (You'll definitely need the genealogy software program called PAF, and we suggest you download all the forms too, while you're at it.)

5 Click on the link for the file you want to save to your hard disk.

6 When the dialog box appears for you to Open/Save/Run the file, click on the **Save** option. (The options in the dialog box or window that opens will depend on the file type and also on the browser software you're using – see example screenshots below).

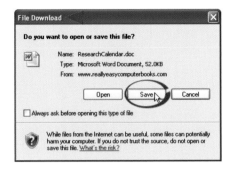  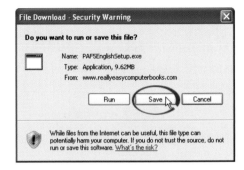

TIP: DOWNLOADING DOCUMENT FILES

When clicking on a link to a Word document or PDF file, the document may open in a separate browser window. To download to your computer you need to click on **File**, then on **Save As…**

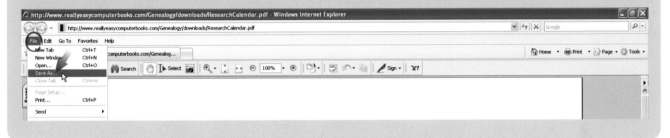

7 In the **Save As** dialog box that opens, click on the **Create New Folder** icon to create a new folder for storing your genealogy work.

8 In the little **New Folder** renaming box that appears at the end of the list of folders in My Documents, type the folder name **Genealogy** and press ⌨Enter⏎ on your keyboard to give the new folder its correct name.

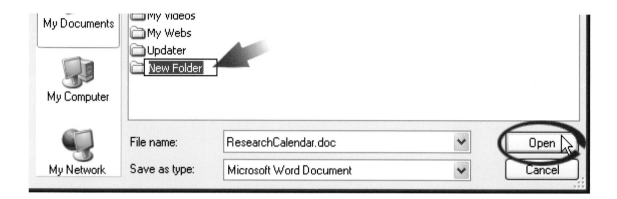

9 Next, click on the **Open** button (screenshot above) to send the folder named Genealogy up to the **Save in:** window.

10 Click on the **Save** button at the bottom right of the **Save As** dialog box to save the file to your Genealogy folder.

11 Tick that item off on the checklist on page 10.

12 Repeat this process for each of the files listed in the checklist, including the two software applications – Personal Ancestral File (PAF) and Adobe Reader.

INSTALL THE GENEALOGY SOFTWARE CALLED PAF

1 Follow the installation instructions in the document **Installing PAF** that you have downloaded from our website, and install the software in preparation for Chapter 2.

THE NEXT STEP

Once you've gathered all your tools of the trade, and in particular the items in the download list on page 10, as well as some folders to start filing your documents, it'll be time to move on to the next chapter and start building your family tree.

2 Starting your family tree

WHAT DETAILS TO RECORD

The minimum basic information you'll be looking for throughout your genealogical project will be each person's:

- full names; date and place of birth
- date and place of marriage, if married
- full names of spouse(s)
- full names of any children
- full names of parents
- date and place of deaths of any of the above

In genealogy terms these are known as *vital details*. Depending on your focus, you may also want to include various other kinds of information as well.

THE STARTING POINT: YOURSELF

Your ancestral family tree project starts with none other than yourself. It then moves back in time to your parents, then their parents (your grandparents) and so on through your lineage.

WHY START WITH YOURSELF?

There are several good reasons for this:

- You probably know more about yourself than anyone else does, so the information you fill in about yourself will most likely be fairly complete and also pretty accurate.
- In the weeks and months ahead you'll be interviewing family members to find out about their own life details, and for that you'll use a checklist of useful questions to ask. By first doing something similar for your own personal details you'll get some valuable practice and also find out which information is easy to remember or obtain, and which information may need additional probing and detective work to uncover or verify.
- By starting with yourself you can add as much detail as you wish and build up your own autobiography about your life. Not only will this serve as a useful document for your own descendants in the future, but it will also give you a real feel of what it's like to try to remember the important things in one's life, such as accomplishments, disappointments, hardships, challenges, and so on. Then, when you're interviewing other family members – parents, grandparents, uncles, aunts, or whoever is available to be interviewed – you can be more sensitive to what they may feel is very personal and perhaps not so easily shared with a younger member of the wider family. This will hone your interviewing skills and help you to document as useful a profile as possible for each individual.

CITING YOUR SOURCES

With every piece of information you record, you'll need to note where you obtained it, with specific detailed references. This is referred to as *citing your sources*. Citing the sources of your information is important to genealogists because:

- It can help one judge the accuracy of the information. When you share your family tree or family history with others, they will most likely want to know where you found the information. Citing your sources is also particularly important if you intend to publish your family tree or family history.
- If you find information that conflicts with what you already have in your family tree data, knowing the source of your original data can help you refer back and determine which information is most likely to be more accurate.
- If you later come across some new details, you can refer back to your original source and see if there is any other information there that you had missed the first time.

VALIDATING YOUR FINDINGS

Filling in the vital details about oneself and one's family unit is very often based on what we already 'know' – from memory, from what we've been told by our parents, and so on. But how much of it has actually been *validated* by means of an original document, such as a birth certificate, marriage certificate, and so on? This brings us to the very important issue of the *nature* of the source of your information.

There are essentially two kinds of sources from which you can obtain information: *primary* sources and *secondary* sources. A primary source is considered to be the most reliable source of information.

PRIMARY AND SECONDARY SOURCES OF INFORMATION

A primary source is a record that was created at the time of an event, by someone who witnessed or at least had a reasonably valid basis for knowing the details of the event. For example, a marriage certificate is documented at the time of the marriage; so it would be a primary source for obtaining the date and place of a marriage and the full names of the wedding couple.

If someone tells you about an event they personally experienced in their life, then that too would be considered a primary source of information about that event. So, your recorded interview with an uncle about his own life would be a primary source for you *about your uncle*; but not a primary source for other people mentioned by your uncle in that interview.

A secondary source would be a record that was created quite some time after the event had taken place (when memories may no longer have been so crystal-clear), or by a person who did not actually witness the event. In the example of a marriage certificate, the document is issued at the time of the marriage, so it would be considered to be a primary source for the marriage details. The certificate also states the dates of birth of the marriage partners. However, these details are noted several decades after the births took place. So although the birth dates do appear on the marriage certificate, the certificate would be considered a *secondary* source for this particular piece of information. A primary source for names and birth dates would be the original *birth* certificates.

In this way, some genealogical sources can act as both primary and secondary sources, depending on which piece of information one is looking at. Regardless of whether your information is from a primary or secondary source, always document the source for future reference.

GATHER YOUR PRIMARY SOURCE DOCUMENTS TOGETHER

Your own knowledge of your birth date and place is, by genealogical standards, considered to be a primary source for your own vital birth details, because it's your own birth, not someone else's. Even so, it's a good idea to get into the habit – right from the beginning – of specifying the sources of the information you have gathered. Having your primary source documents at hand for your own family is a good place to start this important habit. If you can't lay your hands on all of these certificates right now, then at least try to find some of them to use in the procedures that will follow.

Dig out these documents for each member of your immediate family:

✓ Tick off in the white space when found	Father	Mother	Child 1	Child 2	Child 3
• Original birth certificate, or an official copy					
• If baptized, the baptism certificate					
• If married, the marriage certificate					

The next step will be to start recording your own family unit's vital details. We strongly recommend that you do this by means of PAF, the free computer software program designed specifically for genealogy work, and which you will already have downloaded and installed. If you wish, you can make use of paper forms and charts too; these you would fill in by hand, or in some cases by using a word-processing program such as Microsoft Word. However, specialized genealogy software makes the task so much easier, with several other significant benefits too.

SOME OF THE BENEFITS OF USING GENEALOGY SOFTWARE

- You can store the details of thousands of individuals in the one software program.
- You need record a person's details only once, not over and over again in different forms and charts. By typing a person's details just once, and their relationship to another family member, the software can generate various reports and charts for you – including the family tree (pedigree) chart – in a number of different formats.
- At the click of a mouse button you can swiftly move to a new screen to view the pedigree chart of a different ancestor, or details of their family group. You can navigate like this to wherever you want to be in your ancestral family tree – for example, showing the same individual as a parent with a spouse in one view, or a child with siblings in another, and so on.
- Most good genealogy computer programs can export your data into a file format named GEDCOM (**Ge**nealogical **Da**ta **Com**munication), making it possible to share your digital information electronically, by e-mail or via websites, with other genealogists who may have an interest in your family's ancestry but may not have the same brand of software as you. GEDCOM provides an excellent and efficient way for you and others to fill in the gaps in their family trees in this way. It was developed by the creators of PAF software.

START USING PERSONAL ANCESTRAL FILE (PAF)

1 On your computer Desktop, find and double-click on the 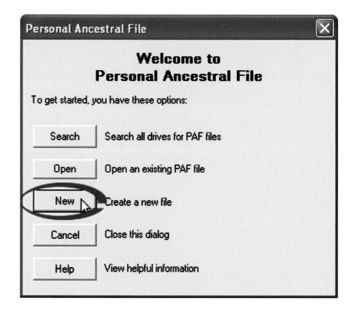 **PAF shortcut icon** to load the program.

2 In the **Welcome** dialog box that opens, click on **New** to create a new family tree ancestral file.

3 In the **Create New Family File** dialog box that opens, click on the ⬝ **down** arrow at the right of the **Save in:** folder window to browse to the **Genealogy** folder you created in My Documents (see Chapter 1), so that **Genealogy** now appears in the **Save in:** window.

4 In the **File name:** window near the bottom, type in a suitable file name, e.g. **HooleFamilyTree**.

5 Click on **Save**.

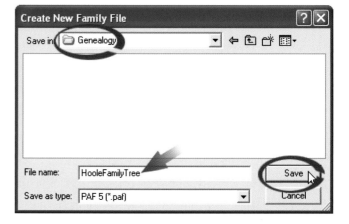

6 In the little **Personal Ancestral File** dialog box that opens the first time you use PAF, click on **Yes**. (In future, when you type in any data and press ⏎, the cursor will move to the next data entry field.)

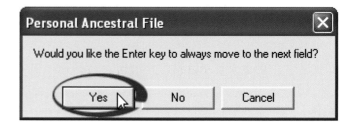

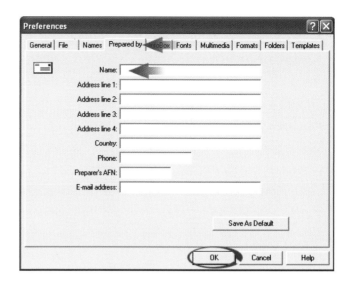

7 In the **Preferences** dialog box that opens with the **Prepared by** tab selected, enter the name and other details of the person who will be typing in all the ancestral data (presumably yourself), and leave the other preference tabs as they are for now. (You can always set other preferences later, once you are more familiar with PAF and its various options.)

8 Click on **OK** to open the next window for entering ancestral data.

A blank chart will open with the Family tab selected. Note that once you've created the new file, the PAF file name will be displayed on the top Title bar.

The first person whose details you enter will automatically be allocated Record Identification Number (RIN) 1. Therefore, for your own family tree, you should start typing your own vital details first. But before you start recording personal details, you need to know about the standard formats used in genealogy to record details.

ALWAYS USE THE STANDARD GENEALOGICAL RECORDING CONVENTIONS

DON'T INVENT YOUR OWN CONVENTIONS OR ABBREVIATIONS From the beginning, be sure to use the formats most commonly used by genealogists, and don't try to invent your own. The reason is simple: when you reach the point where you want to exchange research results with others (so that you can add missing details to your own information base), or share your family history in published form, it will be important that you 'talk the same language' as other genealogists. Otherwise confusion or misunderstanding can creep in, along with the resultant inaccuracies. So, stick with convention.

Here's how to record details for your family tree records.

Individuals' names

- **Sequence:** Record the first name first, then the other given names, with the surname last
- **Surnames:** Capitalize surnames, and place them last: e.g. Cheryl Elizabeth FRENCH. This helps to clarify which of the names is the person's family name
- **Maiden names:** For married women, always use the maiden name (surname at birth). If the maiden name is unknown, never use the married name in its place. Show the first name(s) followed by two forward slashes / / to indicate that the maiden name is unknown: e.g. Cheryl Elizabeth / /

- **Nicknames:** Show a nickname in quotes: e.g. Cheryl 'Cherie' Elizabeth FRENCH
- **Adopted or intentionally changed names:** Show the original name in brackets, preceded by 'a.k.a.' (also known as): e.g. Darren Luther SMITH (a.k.a. Darren Luther BURBANK)
- **Titles:** Include professional titles: e.g. Dr Cheryl Elizabeth FRENCH
- **Accuracy:** Record surnames exactly as you find them. Don't change them to what you think the correct spelling should be. Names were often misspelt due to illiteracy, transcription errors, or misunderstanding what was heard. Record every variation you find too. e.g. Smith, Smyth, Smithe may all represent the same individual; so this should be recorded as: Darren Luther SMITH/SMYTH/SMYTHE. Sometimes surnames were deliberately changed for political or social reasons, possibly when immigrating to a new country. If you know the original spelling, record that version first, followed by the later version(s) used

Dates

- **Sequence and format:** Use the European standard sequence: day, Month, year (dd Mmm yyyy) – one or two digits for the day, three characters for the month (first letter a capital) and four digits for the year – e.g. 2 Feb 1945 or 24 Mar 1918. Most genealogical software can correctly interpret and sort dates in this form, with the months abbreviated as follows:
  Jan Feb Mar Apr May Jun Jul Aug Sep Oct Nov Dec
- **Approximate dates:** Show these with a prefix: abt (short for 'about') or ca. or c. (abbreviation of the Latin word 'circa', meaning 'around' or 'about'): e.g. abt Feb 1945 or ca. Feb 1945 or c. Feb 1945
    - If you don't know the exact date but can establish a range of dates between which the event occurred, then use the abbreviation bet. (short for 'between'), with a hyphen between the two dates. e.g. bet. 12 Jan 1957 – 14 Feb 1957
    - When dates are shown in numerals only, in North America the month is shown first (04/06 would be Apr 6); in Europe and the former colonies it is the day that is usually shown first (04/06 or 4/6 would be 4 Jun). Always record dates exactly as you see them. If you are not sure in which way the recorded date should be interpreted, you might want to add a comment in the Notes to indicate how you think it should be interpreted, preferably with a comment to substantiate your reasoning

Geographical areas

- **Sequence:** List places accurately, proceeding from the smallest to the largest geographic area: e.g. Leeds, West Yorkshire, England, United Kingdom

Abbreviations

- Don't make up your own abbreviations. Use genealogical standards such as **b** for born, **d** for died and **m** for married; also **gg** for great great grandparent, **ggg** for great great great grandparent (a more comprehensive list of standard abbreviations and terms is given on our website)

ENTER YOUR OWN VITAL DETAILS

1 With the **Family** view window open, double-click in the **blue text box** that is highlighted near the top left of the window, to open the **Add Individual** dialog box which will have the cursor flashing in the **Full name:** text window.

2 Type your full names, with your surname in capital letters, then press Enter.

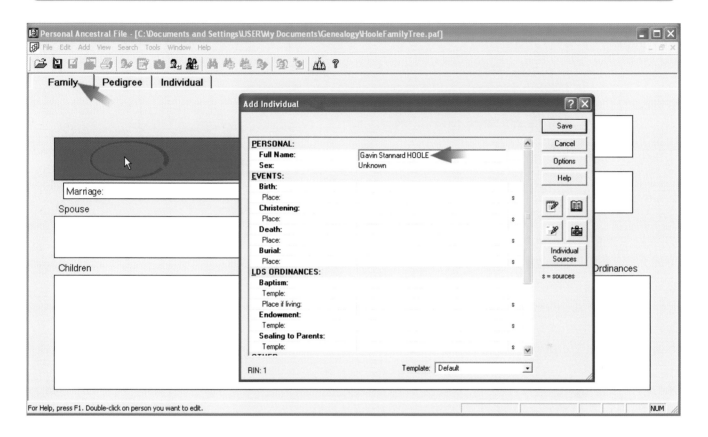

TIP: FORMATTING SURNAMES AUTOMATICALLY

You can set PAF to show surnames in UPPER CASE (capital letters) on screens and reports automatically, and you can also change other preferences. On the Menu bar of the main PAF screen, click on **Tools > Preferences**, and in the **Preferences** dialog box that opens, click on the **Names** tab. Click in the check-box next to **Capitalize surnames on screens and reports**, as well as any other options of your choice. Click on **OK** to change the defaults to your selected preferences.

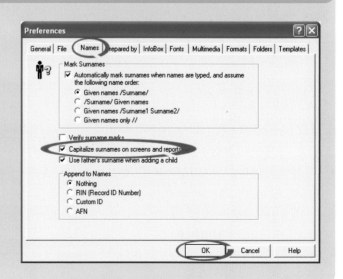

3 Press 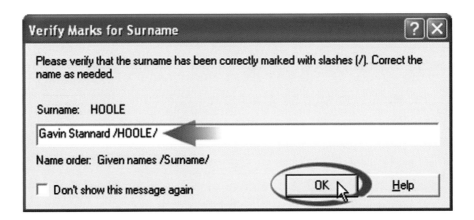 and the **Verify Marks for Surname** dialog box will open.

4 If you're satisfied that the name shown between the two forward slashes is the correct surname, click on **OK** to accept it. If not, click in the name box and type any corrections.

5 Click on **OK** to return to the **Add Individual** dialog box.

TIP: TYPING SPECIAL CHARACTERS IN NAMES

To type a special character in a name – e.g. the **é** in André – with the **Add Individual** dialog box open, click on the **Options** button on the right, then on **Symbol....** Scroll as necessary to find the symbol you require, click on that symbol, then click on **Insert**. (An alternative shortcut to the Symbol box is to press the keyboard F7 button.)

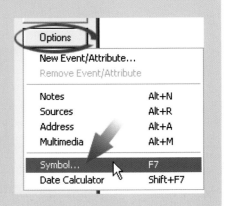

---

6 Click on the little ▾ **down** arrow opposite **Sex:** and click on your gender from the drop-down menu that opens. (If you type the first letter of the gender – e.g. **M** for Male, **F** for Female – PAF will automatically select the correct gender for you, without your having to click on the **down** arrow.)

7 Press Enter and the cursor will jump to the **Birth:** field.

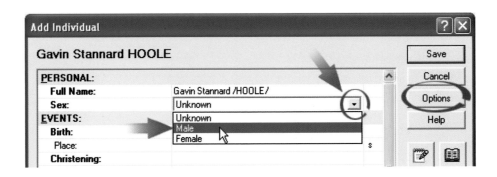

8   Type your **date of birth** using the standard conventions on page 18 – e.g. 17 Nov 1940. (Note that no matter how you type the date, PAF will convert it to the proper format, but it's best to get into the habit of entering it in the standard way.)

9   Press 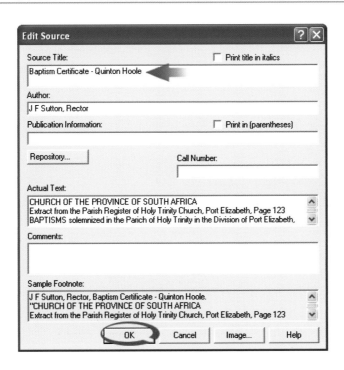 (or) to move to the next field, **Place:** (of birth).

10 Type in the birth place, in the sequence from smallest to largest location, with a comma separating each – e.g. Town, County or Province, Country.

TIP: ENTER YOUR SOURCE REFERENCES AS YOU GO

It's a good idea to add your source references as you enter each item, to avoid having to go back and do it later.

11 Click on the small **s** to the right of (Birth) **Place:** and then on the button that is displayed.

12 In the **Select Source** dialog box that opens, click on the **New** tab at the bottom to open the **Edit Source** dialog box.

13 Type the title of the source document – e.g. **Birth Certificate: (your name)**.

14 Type in any other details you wish to add, related to that source, and press the key to move to the next text field. (An asterisk will now appear (*s) to indicate that there is a source citation for that item.)

15 Repeat Step 13 for each field of the Edit Source box you wish to type into, then click on **OK**.

16 In the **Select Source** dialog box, click on **Close**.

17 Back in the **Add Individual** dialog box, press and continue adding more information and source citations as applicable.

18 If you wish to add other attributes/events that are not in the default list, click on the **Options** button on the right of the dialog box, then click on **New Event/Attribute...** (see screenshot below left).

19 From the list that opens, click on the item you want to add, then on **Select**.

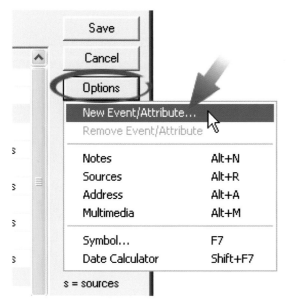

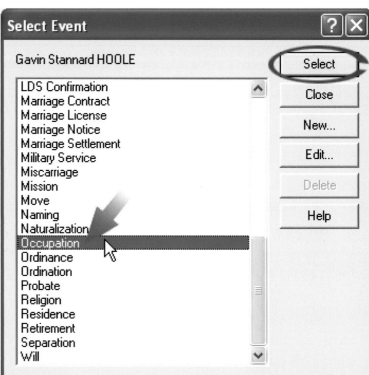

20 When done, click on **Save** to close the Add Individual dialog box and return to the **Family** view window with your name and vital details now shown.

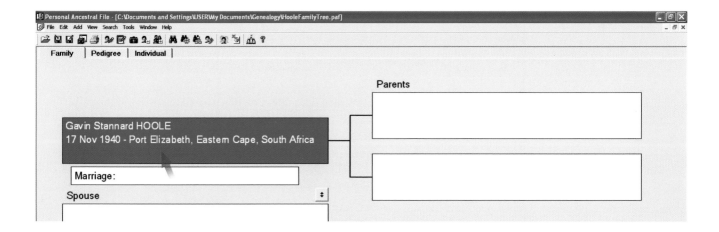

TIP: YOU CAN CUSTOMIZE YOUR DATA INPUT TEMPLATE

The Individual and Marriage screens are currently set to the default PAF template. They may contain data entry fields that you'll never use, or exclude fields you'd like to use quite often. PAF therefore allows you to set up your own customized templates to suit your personal needs. To create your own template(s), on the PAF Menu bar click on **Tools**, then on **Preferences**. In the **Preferences** dialog box that opens, click on the **Templates** tab and follow the prompts. For a more detailed explanation of the procedure, download our free **Creating PAF templates** document from our website, or use the PAF Help features explained at the end of this chapter.

TIP: PAF'S RELIGIOUS TERMINOLOGY CAN BE DISABLED

The Personal Ancestral File software was developed, and is offered free, by the Church of Jesus Christ of Latter Day Saints. It includes terminology and data fields pertaining to that religion. If some of these terms do not apply to you, you can, if you wish, hide Latter Day Saints ordinance fields. In the Menu bar at the top, click on **Tools** > **Preferences** to open the **Preferences** dialog box. Click on the **General** tab and click in the little white checkbox next to **Use LDS data** in order to de-select that option. To change any other default settings too, click on the applicable tab(s) at the top of the box (e.g. **Formats** tab to change date and other entry formats).

ADD ANY MARRIAGE DETAILS

1 Right-click in the box below your name, and click on **Add...**.

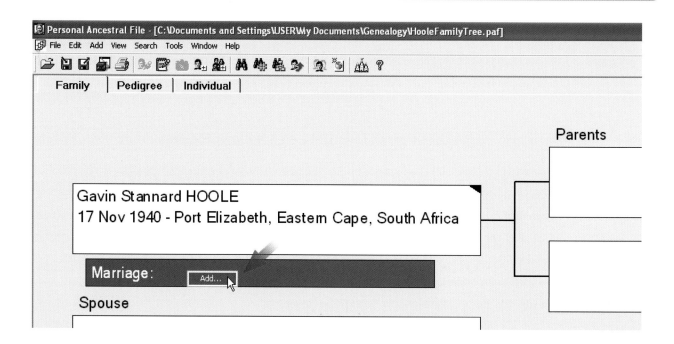

TIP: KNOWING WHAT TO TYPE INTO A FIELD

Usually when you see a field's name such as **Marriage:** the data to be typed into that field is the **date** of the marriage, not the spouse's name, or the place of the wedding. The same applies to such labels as **Birth:, Baptism:, Death:** and so on. It's the **date** that's called for.

---

2 In the **Edit Marriage** dialog box that opens, type in the marriage **date** and press ⏎ to move to the next field; then type the place of the marriage.

3 Click on the small **s** to the right of the (Marriage) **Place:** text window and then on the ⓢ button that comes into view.

4 Follow Steps 12 to 16 in the previous topic's yellow box to enter the source (e.g. Marriage Certificate details).

5 If there was a divorce, click in the little check-box next to **Divorced**.

6 Click on **Save**.

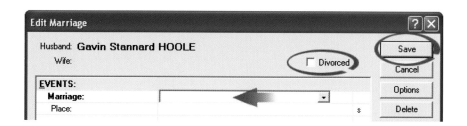

7 To add the spouse's details, double-click in the box below the word **Spouse** and enter the details in the same way as you did for your own name.

8 Click on **Save**.

9 A new dialog box opens at this point. To link the new spouse to the individual shown above, be sure to click on **Yes** in this new dialog box.

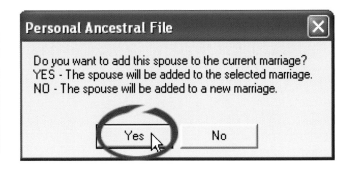

The spouse will now be shown in the box below the individual in the primary position of the Family view screen, and is linked to the current marriage.

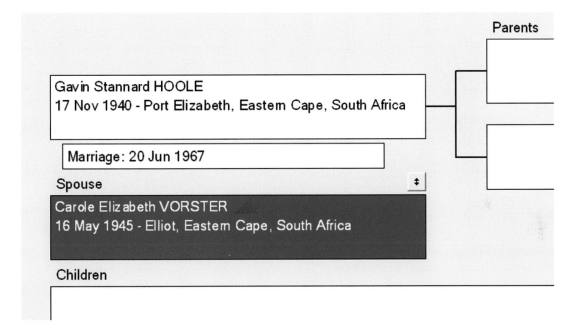

ADD A SECOND MARRIAGE, IF APPLICABLE

1 On the Menu bar, click on **Add**, then on **Spouse...**.

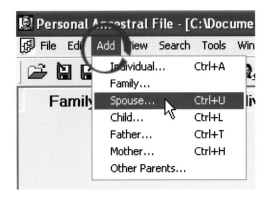

In the **Add or Select Individual** dialog box, click on **Add New Individual** and follow the procedure for adding a new individual. (The **Other Marriages...** button will now appear on the Family view screen; it can be clicked on to view all marriages and to select a different spouse to be displayed on the screen.)

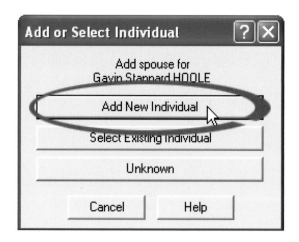

ADD ANY CHILDREN'S DETAILS

REMINDER: ADD CHILDREN IN ORDER OF BIRTH DATE

For more than one child, remember to add the children in their sequence of birth, beginning with the eldest child.

1   In the same **Family** view window, double-click in the box below the word **Children**.
2   In the **Add or Select Individual** dialog box that opens, click on **Add New Individual** (if this is the first time this individual is being entered into PAF – see note below).

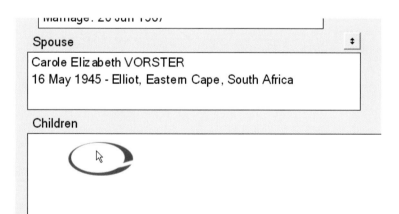

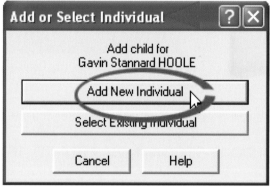

TIP: SELECTING AN EXISTING INDIVIDUAL

When you enter a person's details into PAF, you need do this only once. They will then automatically be stored in the PAF database for future access and editing as necessary. If you wish to add that person as a relative in a particular family, you simply click on the **Select Existing Individual** button (screenshot above), and you won't need to re-type that person's name and details. Instead, you can click on their name.

3 In the **Add child for (individual's name)** dialog box that opens, add the child's details (name, sex, date and place of birth, etc.) as you did for each of the child's parents, and enter the source for each field as well.

4 Click on **Save**.

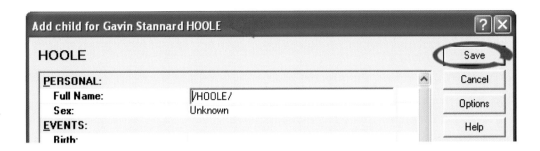

5 In the next dialog box that opens, if you wish to add a second child, click on **Yes** and repeat steps 1 to 4; otherwise click on **No**.

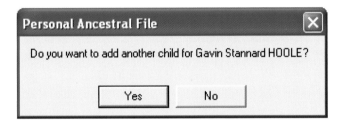

NOTE: PAF HAS THREE VIEWING OPTIONS

You can change the viewing window according to your needs, by clicking on the appropriate tab at the top left of the PAF window – Family, Pedigree or Individual.

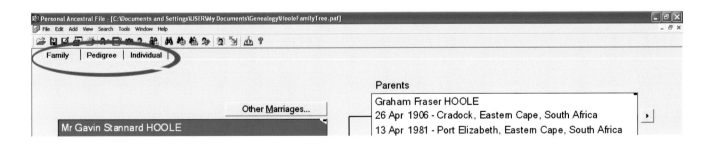

WORKING IN PAF'S FAMILY AND PEDIGREE VIEW WINDOWS

- **To view/edit** an individual's details or marriage details: double-click in the applicable box (individual's Name or Marriage box).
- **To move** to the next generation in time: click on the ⬆ **back** in time or ⬇ **forward** in time arrow.
- **To move a person** to the primary (top left) position: right-click on their name or name-box, and click on **Move to Primary**.
- **To swap positions** between the primary position person and their spouse, click on the ⬍ **switch positions** button (Family view only).
- **To access a menu** of actionable tasks for an individual, right-click on their name or name-box.
- **To view/edit** an individual's notes, photo or sound/video clip: click on the black symbol in the top right corner of the individual's name box, then click on the item you wish to view/edit. (Symbols vary in shape or combination according to what extras have been added to an individual's database. ⌐ indicates there are notes for this person; ⌐ shows there is multimedia for this individual; and ⌐ indicates both notes and multimedia.)

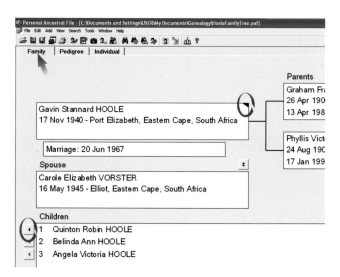

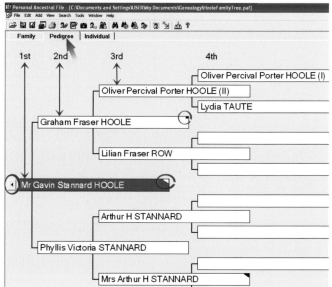

WORKING IN PAF'S INDIVIDUAL VIEW SCREEN

PAF's Individual view lists every individual in your PAF database. This is very useful for finding an individual, either by surname or by their RIN reference – in either ascending or descending order.

- **To sort by surname**, click on the **Full Name** heading at the top of the names list; to reverse the order, click again on the heading.
- **To sort by RIN**, follow the same procedure with the **RIN** heading.
- **To view or edit** an individual's details, double-click on their name.

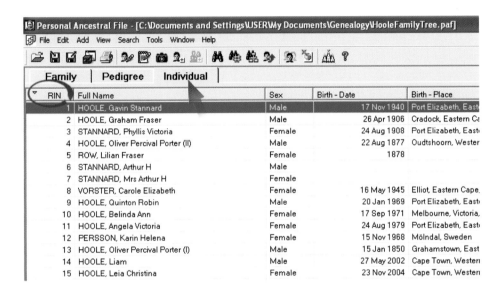

TIP: OPENING A CHART FOR AN INDIVIDUAL IN THE LIST

You can click on a name in the Individual view list, then on either the Family tab or the Pedigree tab, and the applicable chart will open with that person displayed in the primary position.

DELETING AN INDIVIDUAL

Perhaps it turns out that Uncle Fred wasn't a real uncle after all, but just a close family friend who should not have been included in your family tree. You can delete an individual or a marriage from any one of the three view screens, as follows:

1. Click on the name of the individual you want to delete.
2. On the Menu bar, click on **Edit**, then on **Delete Individual**. (Alternatively, in the Individual view screen, you could also click on the person's name and press the keyboard [Del] key.)

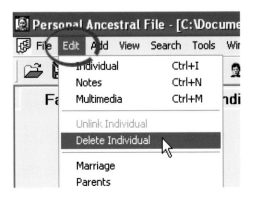

PRINTING REPORTS

With PAF you can print a wide range of charts, lists and reports, customized according to your needs.

1 On the Menu bar click on **File**, then on **Print Reports...** (or press `Ctrl` + `P`).

2 In the **Reports and Charts** dialog box, click on **each tab** to explore the various reports and options available.

3 Click on **Preview** to see what the report looks like.

4 Click on **Print** when you're ready to print a hard copy.

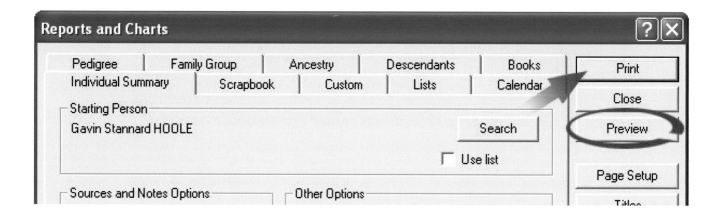

NOTE: YOU CAN ALSO PRINT BLANK FORMS

Some of the tabs offer the option to print a blank form that can be used for filling in by hand. This is particularly useful when you interview family members or do research away from home without a laptop, and need to add new individuals to your database by hand.

BACK UP YOUR PAF DATA

It is not necessary to save your PAF data before exiting PAF, because PAF automatically saves everything when you enter data and click on Save in the dialog box. But backing up your file is essential. PAF will remind you every time you close the program. (The number of times you can open and close PAF before you are reminded to back up can be changed or even disabled in Tools/Preferences/Backup prompt frequency.)

CREATE AN OFF-COMPUTER BACK-UP EVERY TIME YOU EDIT It is essential that you create a back-up copy located off your computer's hard drive every time you've finished adding to or editing your PAF file. If your hard drive fails and you have no back-up, you can lose many, many hours (or even years) of valuable work.

Remember, a back-up on the same computer is useless if the computer 'crashes'. Your backup *must* be on a separate drive – either a CD, a DVD, an external drive, a different computer or on a Web server on the Internet. In the event of computer failure, once your system has been repaired you can restore your PAF file from the backup copy.

Creating a backup copy

1 Insert a floppy disk or rewritable CD or DVD, or connect an external drive or computer network to your system.
2 On the Menu bar, click on **File**, then on **Backup...**.
3 In the **Back Up File To...** dialog box that opens, click on the little ▾ **down** arrow (screenshot below left) to browse to and click on the **destination drive** to which you want to save the backup.
4 PAF will generate the type of file (.zip) and the correct file name.
5 Click on **Backup** (screenshot below right) to start the backing-up process.

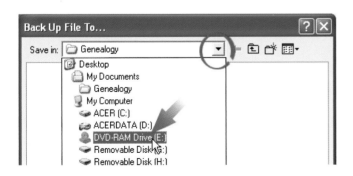

Restoring from your backup file

If you ever need to restore your data after a computer crash, here's how:

1 On the PAF Menu bar, click on **File**, then on **Restore…**.

2 In the **Restore File From…** dialog box that opens, follow the steps as explained in step 2 of the backing-up procedure to browse to the disk/drive and folder where your backup file is saved.

3 Click on the **.zip** backup file, then on the **Restore** button to execute the Restore process. (Your restored file will open in PAF, ready for editing.)

NOTE: RESTORING WITH AN EXISTING PAF FILE OPEN

It doesn't matter whether you have a blank screen open in PAF, or another PAF file open. PAF will restore the backup file and open that one in PAF immediately it's been restored.

BECOMING MORE PROFICIENT WITH PAF

PAF offers much more than can be covered in a genealogy beginner's book such as this. We therefore suggest that you refer to the PAF Help and Lessons features (see next two topics) in order to build your know-how on getting the most out of PAF, so that developing your computerized family tree can be a breeze.

Getting on-screen topic-related help

Pressing the F1 keyboard button brings up a PAF Help screen relevant to what is displayed on the screen at the time.

Help with a particular dialog box:

1 With a dialog box open and the cursor flashing in the field on which you need guidance, press ▢F1 on the keyboard; a help topic box will pop up with an explanation for that item.

2 To close the help topic box, press ▢Esc or click anywhere in the open dialog box.

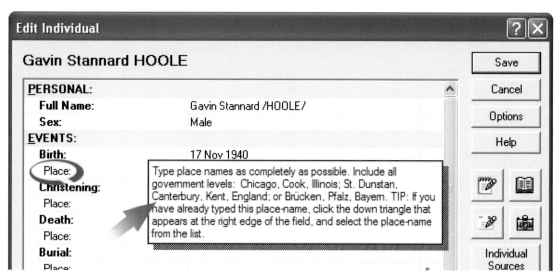

The help topic box that pops up when F1 is pressed while the cursor is flashing in the Birth Place field

Help with a PAF window:

1 With no dialog box open, press the keyboard button **F1**; the PAF **Help** box will open with Tips in the right-hand panel that relate to the PAF view that is in use (Family, Pedigree or Individual).

2 To view a list of subject headings, click on the **Contents** tab and then on the **+** **plus** sign next to an item in order to see its sub-headings.

3 Click on a **sub-heading** and the relevant help notes will be displayed in the pane on the right.

4 If you need more guidance of how to use the PAF Help feature, in the **Contents** list click on the item, **Using the online help**.

5 Another method of getting help is to click on the **Index** tab of the Help window, and type into the **Keyword** box a word related to the topic on which you need help.

6 In the list that is displayed below the keyword box, double-click on the item that matches your need.

7 In the **Topics Found** window that opens, click on the topic that best describes your query, then click on the **Display** button to bring the information into view in the right-hand pane.

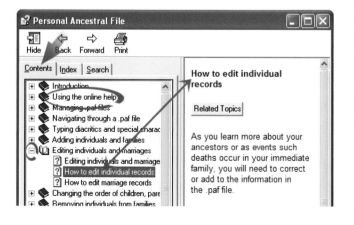

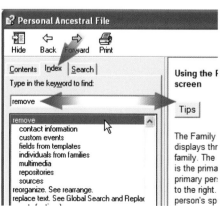

Learning more about PAF

Personal Ancestral File has quite an awesome range of capabilities which we recommend you explore once you've become familiar with the basics already covered in this chapter. Besides the Help options already explained, the two main PAF user information sources are the on-screen Lessons feature and the User's Guide document of nearly 200 pages.

On-screen Lessons

1   On the PAF Menu bar click on **Help**, then on **Lessons** and wait while the Lessons window opens in your Internet browser (e.g. Internet Explorer).

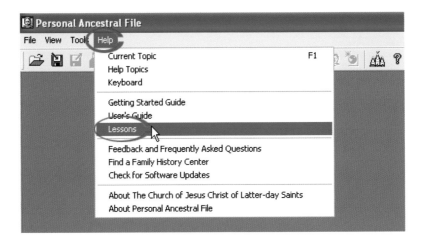

2   At the bottom of the **Lessons** panel on the left of the browser window, click on the **next** or **back** button to navigate between the lessons.

3 Click on the **<u>Show Me</u>** link (where available) to follow an animated instruction of the procedures described; the animation will open in a new window overlaying your browser's main window. (You will need to have JAVA installed in order to view the Show Me animated tutorials.)

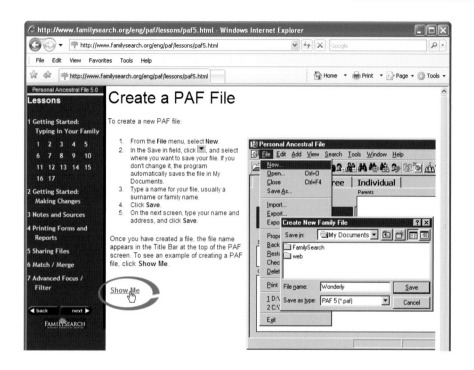

4 To close the animated demo click on **Quit** or on the ⊠ **Close** button at the top of the overlaying window.

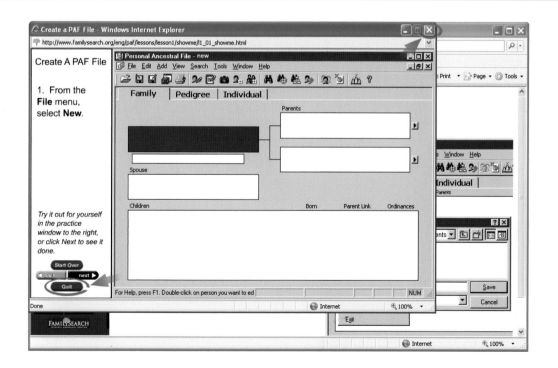

STARTING YOUR FAMILY TREE

TIP: WORK THROUGH ALL THE PAF LESSONS

Working through the PAF Lessons one by one in this way, and referring to the printout of the User's Guide, will give you a good understanding of how the program works and the correct methods of entering data. This time investment now will save you time later.

User's Guide

1 On the Menu bar, click on **Help**, then on **User's Guide** and wait for the PDF document to load. (You'll need to have Adobe Reader installed in order to view PDF files.)

2 In the left-hand Bookmarks panel, click on **Table of Contents** heading to open the very detailed list of contents.

3 In the nine-page Table of Contents that opens, scroll as necessary and click on a **topic** to go straight to the page on which that item is covered.

TIP: CHECK OCCASIONALLY FOR PAF SOFTWARE UPDATES

Although PAF software is not updated very frequently, it's still a good idea to check for program updates every now and again. On the Menu bar, simply click on **Help**, then on **Check for Updates**…. You need to be connected to the Internet to check for updates.

THE NEXT STEP

Once you've recorded the essential pieces of information for each person – their vital details and the sources of those details – you can start to expand your records with any extra information that interests you, in order to develop a family history. The extent of this additional research will, of course, depend on your chosen objective and focus as covered in Chapter 1.

The next chapter will explain how to expand your family tree to earlier generations and find details that can be developed into a family history.

3 Developing your family history

This is a good time to start documenting your own life story. In so doing, you will also get a feel for the interviewing process of gathering information about other family members and their lives, as covered in the next chapter. Consider this to be like writing your autobiography, in as much or as little detail as you wish. If you make it interesting and detailed enough it could become a personal profile that you can hand down to your own descendants, for them to use to keep the family tree details and family history alive for generations to come.

As you make notes about yourself and your immediate family members (any spouse and children), record them into your PAF files as explained below.

ENTERING NOTES AND OTHER INFORMATION INTO PAF

You can add various extra items to a person's profile to increase the interest value of your family tree and to record background details for reports, scrapbooks, and the like. It is also possible to add multimedia (a photo, a sound file such as speech, or a video clip), but you will need to have the digital file stored on your computer or on a CD/DVD.

---

1 First, with the **Family** view tab selected, double-click on the person's **name box** to open the **Edit Individual** dialog box, and note the group of click-on buttons to the right.

Adding notes:

2 Click on the **note pad** icon (or press Alt + N), type your notes, then click on **Save**.

Viewing all information sources you've recorded:

3 Click on the **open book** icon (or press Alt + R)

Adding or editing contact information:

4 Click on the **envelope** button (or press Alt + A), type the details, then click on **OK**.

Adding a photo, sound file or video clip:

5 Click on the **camera** icon, then on **Add**.

6 Click on the little ▾ **down** arrow to select the type of item (photo, sound, video), then browse to find and select the file on your computer, and click on **Open**.

7 In the spaces provided, type in any caption and description you wish to add, then click on **OK**.

8 Click on **Save** in each of the next two dialog boxes that open.

Individual Sources | **Viewing/editing a particular source you've added:**

9 Click on the **Individual Sources** button and click on the particular source you want to view or edit, then click on **Select**.

VIEWING AN INDIVIDUAL'S NOTES OR MULTIMEDIA

The photo of the individual in the primary position (in this case, you) will be displayed in their name box. A tiny black symbol in the top right-hand corner of a person's name box will indicate that additional details are available for that person. To view these:

1 Right-click in the **name box**, and in the drop-down menu (screenshot below right) click on the item you wish to view and it will be displayed in a dialog box.

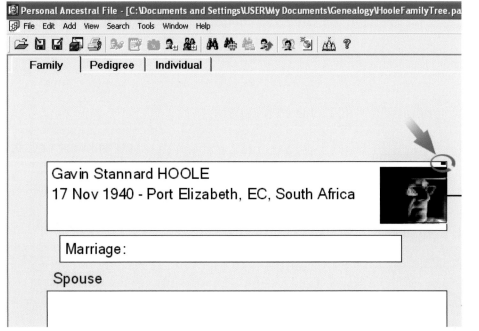

PERSONAL INTERVIEW QUESTIONS

When you start interviewing your relatives one by one, we'll recommend that you use an Interview Questionnaire Checklist (downloadable from our website) to help you cover most of the important areas of each person's life. Below is a list of questions you could use right now to compile your own personal life story. It is based on the Interview Questionnaire Checklist. (You have probably already entered your family's vital details – birth, marriage, death – into PAF, in which case those questions can obviously be skipped for this exercise.)

> **1** Work your way through the questions below and type the answers into your PAF family tree file as explained in the nine steps in the previous topic.
>
> **2** Where you want to type a longer note, such as a short autobiography, type it into a separate document such as a Word file, and use that document as the source you refer to in PAF.

About yourself

❑ Do you know why your given name was selected for you? Were you named after anyone else in your family?

❑ Do your given names include a surname from one of your ancestors? Is there such a tradition in your family?

❑ Besides your given names that you have entered into PAF, do you have any nickname?

❑ Why were you given your nickname?

❑ When and where were you born?

❑ Do you know if there were any special circumstances surrounding your birth? (e.g. born on a train; any medical complications; during a terrible storm; while your parents were on holiday abroad)

❑ Are there any things you can remember about your early childhood?

❑ What school(s) did you attend? Did you finish school?

❑ Did you have any special achievements at school? (academic; head boy or head girl; school prefect; sports team captain; music; arts, etc.)

❑ Did you go on to college/university, or do any further courses after high school? If so, what did you study? Did you receive a university or college degree?

❑ Have you done any military service; served in any wars? Which particular service were you in, and which regiment or unit? Did you serve anywhere abroad? Where?

❑ What do you do for a living?

❑ What other occupations have you had? Which was the most rewarding occupation?

❑ Do you have any pets? What are they, and what are their names?

❑ Did you immigrate/emigrate? From where to where? Did you travel by ship/plane/train?

❑ Are there any events or aspects of your life that have really meant a lot to you?

❑ If you were to write your own eulogy, how would you like to sum up your life or describe yourself?

About your parents and your siblings

❑ What are your parents' full names? Any nicknames?

❑ When and where were they born?

❑ When and where were they married? Do you know how and where they met each other?

❑ Do you have photographs of your parents?

❑ What are/were their occupations?

❑ If your parents are deceased, how and when did they die, and where are they buried?

❑ Do you have any brothers or sisters? Are they younger or older than you? What are they like? Do you have any childhood memories about them?

❑ What are the full names of these siblings (and any nicknames)?

❑ What is each sibling's birth date and where was each one born?

❑ If any siblings have died, how and when did they die, and where are they buried?

About your grandparents

❑ Do you know or remember any of your grandparents, what they are/were like, or where they lived?

❑ Have your parents told you anything about your grandparents' lives?

❑ If any grandparents have died, do you know how they died, where they died or were buried?

About your spouse

❑ What is your spouse's full name, date and place of birth?

❑ When and where were you married? Did you go away on honeymoon? Where to?

❑ What is/was your spouse's occupation?

❑ If your spouse is deceased, how and when did he/she die, and where is he/she buried?

❑ Did you remarry? What is/was your second spouse's name? (Any other spouses?)

About your children and their families

❑ What are the full names, dates and places of birth of each of your children?

❑ If any of your children have died, how and when did they die, and where are they buried?

❑ Are any of your children married? Where? When?

❑ What are the full names and the birth date and place of each child's spouse?

❑ What are the full names and date and place of birth each child's children (your grandchildren)?

About your family group

❑ Have there been any divorces in the family group? If so, who and what dates?

❑ Were there any adoptions? Who? When? Where?

❑ Do you have any original marriage, birth or death certificates?

❑ Do you have a family Bible? (It was commonplace to record the family births, deaths and marriages inside the family Bible – see next topic.)

❑ Has anyone else in the family previously done any genealogy research? If so, do you know where they can be contacted?

❑ Do you have any family medical history of significance?

BROWSING THROUGH FAMILY ARCHIVES

Family files and archives can be a mine of useful information that you can use to add more details into your family history and your family tree files. Going through family treasures can be a lot of fun too, and can bring back some fond memories and proud moments.

1 Pull out old boxes and files and then go through their contents with an eye to finding any details and information that could then be added to your existing genealogy records.

2 When you find new information, add it to your PAF file; make sure you also file any documents in your file folders.

3 Update your Resource details too.

BOOK: COURTESY THE TAYLOR FAMILY
PHOTOS, DRAWINGS: COURTESY CHERYL SMITH

Examples of what items to look for

- Adoption records
- Anniversary guest books
- Autograph books
- Baby announcements
- Baby books
- Baptism records
- Birth certificate
- Building plans
- Church Confirmation records
- Club/association documents
- Credit statements
- Death announcements
- Death certificates
- Diaries and journals
- Diplomas
- Divorce papers
- Driver's licences
- Employment records
- Family Bibles
- Family business papers
- Family correspondence
- Family histories

- Family needlepoint sampler
- Family pictures
- Family records
- Fire insurance papers
- First papers of citizenship
- Funeral programs
- Graduation records
- Health insurance cards
- Hospital/medical records
- Identity documents
- Immigration identification cards
- Income tax forms
- Last Will & Testament papers
- Life assurance papers
- Magazine subscriptions
- Marriage certificates
- Military awards
- Military discharge papers
- Military draft cards
- Naturalization papers
- Newspaper clippings
- Photo albums

- Previously prepared genealogy records
- Property deeds
- Probate/estate records
- Property tax receipts
- Ration books
- Recorded oral histories
- School enrolments
- School magazines
- School report cards
- Scrapbooks
- Social Security cards
- Trade Union cards
- Travel tickets
- Vehicle insurance papers
- Vehicle registration documents
- Wedding announcements
- Wedding guest books
- Wedding programmes
- Wills and administrations

HANDLE WITH CARE Old books and photographs are fragile and are subject to deterioration over time. They need to be handled with great care to protect them for future generations to enjoy.

TIPS: HANDLING PHOTOGRAPHS, OLD DOCUMENTS, BOOKS, ETC.

- Newspaper clippings are very acidic. To prevent acids from migrating, store clippings in their own folders and never with photographs.
- Our skin gives off acids which could damage photographs, slides, negatives, documents and certificates. Wear white cotton gloves designed for this purpose – found in archival supply stores.
- Use archival tape rather than standard adhesive tape.
- Metal staples and wire paper clips rust; use plastic clips.
- Always use pencil when writing on the backs of documents or photographs. Different inks have acid-causing properties or chemicals in them.
- Never use rubber bands to hold anything together. Rubber is harmful to old documents and can melt in high temperatures, disintegrate and stick to your papers.
- Keep photos and documents away from light. Make copies of the documents you want to show, and display only the copies.
- Use archival storage boxes for printed materials and photographs (constructed from acid-free materials). These boxes are solid and secured in order to resist dust, dirt and light infiltration. Metal-reinforced corners create a secure seam and resist crushing.
- Do not hold photos and documents while viewing them; lay them on a flat surface.
- Store materials in a cool, dry area; never in a hot attic or damp basement.

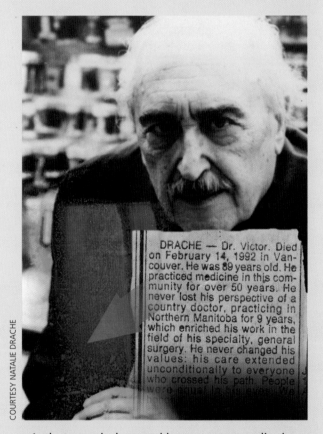

COURTESY NATALIE DRACHE

A photograph damaged by a newspaper clipping

 PROTECT YOUR ARCHIVES FROM DAMAGE Keep your storage boxes and archives well above ground level in case of floods.

This family (below) lost all their old memorabilia and photographs due to flooding and fire in their home in the Philippines. Thankfully, a wedding portrait had been painted by a family member commemorating this couple's special day – now the only remaining image left to their descendants.

COURTESY GRACE CAMASURA

COURTESY PAUL SMITH FAMILY

Autograph book, ca.1880's, with signatures that reveal names and family relationships on every page

COURTESY PAUL SMITH FAMILY

Old family Bible

In earlier generations, records of special family events were often kept inside the family Bible, on pages that were designed specifically for recording marriages, births and deaths. The family Bible shown above records the first birth in 1807. The middle pages of these Bibles often had slots in which to keep photographs safely preserved.

COURTESY REBECCA CHALMERS

Example of a needlepoint sampler

Young girls in your family may have stitched needlepoint 'samplers' which commonly contained a blessing, the letters of the alphabet, her name and either the date she completed the sampler or her date of birth.

COURTESY CHERYL SMITH

Carefully study the old photographs that you uncover and you may recognize a treasure that you inherited, whether it be a necklace, a pocket watch, medals, clothing or an item of furniture. The author found this old photograph in her family archives and was delighted to see that the necklace her grandmother was wearing is the one she herself had inherited as a 13-year-old child.

PLAYING THE GENEALOGICAL DETECTIVE GAME

COURTESY PAUL AND CHERYL SMITH

Old certificates tell of achievements

If you scrounge around you may find old certificates that give you some insight as to what an ancestor was up to in the early years.

COURTESY NATALIE DRACHE

Old clippings, photos and scrap books can reveal a lot

Bits and pieces of information pertaining to a single event can paint a picture of a wedding day, including a voyage on the S.S. Olympic, sister ship of the Titanic, and a year-long honeymoon overseas.

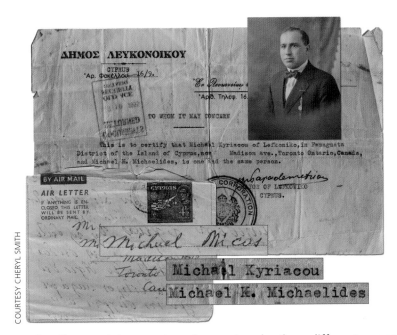

COURTESY CHERYL SMITH

Detective discovery! An ancestor who went under three different surnames!

The author's grandfather had a history shrouded in mystery. However, after his death and the discovery of his diary as well as letters he had received from a family which no one knew he had, new insights came to light. It was determined that at the age of 17 he had left his parents, four sisters and two brothers in a village in Cyprus, travelled the world and ultimately settled in North America in 1907. Telegrams from the Mayor of his village revealed that granddad had two different surnames, yet neither was the name he went by. Unless important facts like these are discovered as you search the records of a relative, you will hit a brick wall as far as finding out anything further relating to your ancestry. This detective work adds to the fun of genealogy.

COURTESY DAVID AND SUZANNE THOMPSON

COURTESY CHERYL SMITH

Clothing fashion in old photos can be a guide to the era

Names and dates were not usually recorded on the backs of old photographs. So if you discover a professionally taken photo such as the one above, it may be a challenge to determine the number of generations portrayed in this image, what the relationships might be and the approximate date. The clothing worn indicates that the photo was probably taken in the late 1800's.

School photograph, late 1800's

With some photo restoration, it should be possible to read the chalk board that the little girl in the front row is holding, which probably holds the key to the name of the school and the exact year the photo was taken. The clothing worn by the girls indicates that the year may be around the late 1800's, which means the author's grandmother and her sisters are probably in the photo.

COURTESY CHERYL, DIANA AND SHANNON

Love letters and other correspondence can provide new insights into the personal lives of one's ancestors

After the author's parents died, she and her sisters discovered a package of letters, newspaper clippings and a wedding photograph at the bottom of their mother's cedar chest. The letters (spanning the years 1940–1942) were from their father, a 25-year-old man serving in the Canadian Air Force, to their mother, a 22-year-old girl from the Prairies. Although the letters are obviously very personal, they did provide a great deal of information such as their mother's physical address at the time, where their father was stationed, and on the personal side, some insight as to how their long-distance relationship endured and sustained itself, the courtship right up to the discussion of the wedding ring and finally the wedding arrangements.

THE NEXT STEP: FILLING IN THE MISSING FAMILY TREE DETAILS

Once you've recorded all the information you can about your immediate family – from within your own family records and storage boxes – you'll probably find there are a lot of gaps that need to be filled, and some interesting questions that your findings have raised. This takes you to your next step in your information-gathering journey: interviewing family members who are still alive – your parents, uncles, aunts, grandparents, and others. In the next chapter you'll learn how to go about this interesting family interviewing process, and you'll learn some tips for doing long-distance 'interviews' with relatives in other towns or countries.

You've already experienced a self-interview in this chapter, so you'll now have a good feel of how the process works. When you interview family members we suggest you use the Interview Questionnaire Checklist that can be downloaded from our website (see page 10). You will also need the Interview Record form that is available from our website. It includes spaces to record the interviewer's name, interview date and venue, and the name of the family member being interviewed. Print additional copies as necessary, ready for all your family interviews.

TIP: WORK BACKWARDS, ONE GENERATION AT A TIME

The safest method for ensuring that you build your family tree with accurate information is to work backwards in time, and to do this one generation at a time. For example, when collecting information about your parents, try to complete that generation – with all the vital details you need about your parents – before you move backwards in time to their parents (your grandparents). If, while researching your parents you happen to come across something of interest or importance about your grandparents, or another generation, then by all means make a note of it for later, but don't start researching all over the place. To remain focused it's best to work with one generation at a time.

4 Researching your wider family

Once you've filled in as much as you can from the resources available within your own family unit it's time to branch out and start working back in time, beginning with your parents.

You'll be asking individual family members to give up an hour or more of their time for you. It's therefore important to plan properly so that they know what it's all about, can feel comfortable about the idea, and can prepare themselves in advance. At the same time, good preparation – along with good interviewing skills – will provide you with the best results for your research.

 INTERVIEW NOW – BEFORE IT'S TOO LATE People age; memories fade. And no one lives forever.

PREPARE FOR YOUR INTERVIEW

1 Go through the work you've done thus far and identify where there is the most missing information, or missing information you feel will be quick and easy to obtain. Use this to decide your priority list of people you wish to interview. (If one's own parents are alive, they are usually the best place to start.)

2 Contact the person to be interviewed and make a firm appointment for the meeting.
  ❑ Explain what it's all about and try to inspire them to look forward to the meeting – for example, by expressing your interest in hearing their favourite stories about their life; or telling them you're keen to hear about your family's past and your own heritage.
  ❑ Tell them it will probably take an hour or more.

3 On your Interview Record sheet fill in the details of the meeting in advance:
  ❑ your name as interviewer;
  ❑ the name of the person being interviewed;
  ❑ the date and venue of the interview.

4 Prepare your tools of the trade to take with you, and tick them off below:
  ❑ printouts of the relevant pedigree charts from PAF, showing the missing vital details you want to complete during the interview;
  ❑ notebooks, pens, pencils, etc;
  ❑ camera (digital or film) or camera phone;
  ❑ sound recorder (audio-tape, digital, or laptop computer – with microphone);

❑ fully-charged batteries and spares for the recorder;

❑ any photographs, documents and family keepsakes you have that may jog the person's memory and stimulate them to provide even more information – this is especially useful when the talking seems to stall.

CONDUCTING THE INTERVIEW

Some tips to help you get the most out of your interview.

- **Put the interviewee at ease:** Let the interviewee feel that this will be a good opportunity to share their knowledge and memories, and not some kind of interrogation. This approach will make the session pleasant for both of you and help to draw out a lot of useful and interesting information. Also, show your appreciation for the time they have agreed to give you for the interview.

- **Ask permission before recording:** If you intend making a sound or video recording of the session, first ask your interviewee if they're happy with that. You can explain that it frees you up to listen carefully to what they say, and that it will help you not to forget anything important.

- **Begin with the familiar:** Ask a question or mention a topic you know the person will be keen to respond to – perhaps an anecdote from the past that you know the interviewee likes to talk about. This will put both of you at ease and open the door to free-flowing information sharing.

- **Seek information, not a 'yes' or a 'no' answer:** Structure your questions in such a way that they elicit the sharing of information, feelings, memories, anecdotes, and so on, not simply a 'yes' or a 'no'. One way to do this is to ensure that the question itself does not contain an answer on which you want confirmation. For example: don't ask, 'So, you were born in Dorset?' Rather ask, 'So, where were you born, and what was it like there in those days?'

- **Try not to interrupt or take over the conversation:** Let the interviewee speak at his or her own pace. Elderly people often need more time than younger folk to gather their thoughts and recall past memories. So if you're interviewing an elderly relative, be patient yet supportive, participating as appropriate while not hogging the conversation. In short, be a good listener.

- **Be sensitive and not pushy:** Some topics may be very sensitive to the interviewee, such as the death of a loved one, or some family history of which they're not too proud. If a question seems to elicit discomfort or a reluctance to answer, this could be a signal that you're treading on touchy ground. Drop the question and move on to something lighter.

- **Use your family items as prompts:** Bringing out some old family photos, newspaper clippings, documents or family heirlooms you've brought with you can be a good way to stimulate a flood of memories and stories from the past, and provide you with new insights you weren't aware of before. Show your interviewee your pedigree chart and how it's taking shape, where the gaps are, and so on. This can inspire a desire to help you further and add more substance to your family history.

- **Try to access family archives:** Family archives can be a very useful source of information. Tactfully ask whether there are any such documents or photo albums you could browse through together with your interviewee. This can open up even more memories and anecdotes and provide you with some details and angles not covered thus far.

- **Browse through their bookshelves:** With permission, pull out what look like older books and flip through the pages. There may be notes inside the covers indicating that the book was a gift to someone, and you can note their name and any birth date given. There may be bookmarks in the form of cards, notes, old travel receipts, or theatre tickets. These could one day serve as links to other information you already have or are looking for.

- **Ask permission before taking any photographs:** You may want to take some photos of the person you're interviewing, or of their home, surroundings or any heirlooms or documents. First ask permission, and offer to provide them with printed copies of the photographs.

- **Keep notes (audio, video or written) of everything you're told:** Sometimes a statement may seem unimportant at the time, or not particularly relevant, yet at some time in the future it may offer a vital clue to a missing piece in your family tree puzzle.

- **Don't overstay your welcome:** Two hours is considered too long. Most people, especially seniors, tire after one hour of concentrated discussion. If the interview is going well and the interviewee is still enthusiastic, then by all means continue – but be sensitive to weariness.

- **Close off with appreciation and gratitude:** Before you grab your things and rush off, show your appreciation for their time, patience and being prepared to share their life with you. Ask if they would like to be kept informed should you later find out some more interesting things about their family. Keep the door open for possible future interviews.

 ASK ABOUT EXISTING FAMILY TREE INFORMATION Genealogy has become very popular in recent times, and so some of the relatives you contact for interviews may already have done their own genealogical research, or may know of a relative who has done so. Such ready-available ancestry information could save you much time and effort, so always remember to ask about this.

UPDATE YOUR FAMILY TREE AFTER EACH INTERVIEW

1   After each interview, update your PAF file from the additional information and vital details you gathered during the interview session.

2   Cross-check details from your interview record and make a note of any discrepancies between the new details gathered and what you already have in your PAF records (e.g. dates, spelling of names, places of birth or marriage).

3   Pursue these discrepancies in order to determine the correct information from some reliable source and rectify any errors in your database.

4   Update your source citations as necessary.

CONTACTING OUT-OF-TOWN RELATIVES
Where you need to obtain input from relatives who live away from your home-town, you'll probably need to do this via telecommunication or mail unless you're planning to take a trip to visit them.

Tips for distance interviewing
- **Interview in person whenever and wherever possible:** Personal information is always best shared in person. And personal interviews give you the opportunity to display your sincerity and trustworthiness about maintaining any confidentiality pertaining to sensitive or highly personal information you receive. If at all possible, take a trip to your relative to do the interview. Alternatively, when you plan a holiday, find out which relatives or friends live in that area and schedule to visit them while you're on vacation.
- **Use telecommunications as the next best option:** As an alternative, if practical, conduct the interview by telephone, which is more personal than by mail. If you have a broadband Internet connection and an instant messaging program, this would also be a good option. If your computer doesn't have MSN Messenger or Windows Messenger installed, Microsoft offers Windows Live Messenger which can be downloaded free at: **http://www.microsoft.com/downloads**. Another very popular instant voice and text messaging program is offered free by Skype. It can be downloaded at **http://www.skype.com**. Using such a program, you can set up an online appointment and interview your relative electronically by voice or text messaging – provided, of course, that they too are likewise Internet-enabled and instant messenger-enabled. If you have a webcam, that's even better; the person you are interviewing can 'see' you while you're conducting the interview via Messenger or Skype.
- **Don't just send out forms to be filled in:** This is a very cold method of trying to obtain ancestry information, and the chances of receiving a detailed and useful response are not good. If written correspondence is the only way, then always contact your interviewee first by telephone and use the same approach as when setting up a face-to-face personal interview. This will make the person comfortable about your motives and genuineness, and will create the all-important initial rapport with your interviewee. You could tell them you'd love to see them in person, but unfortunately you can't, so you'd appreciate some assistance by mail. Then make arrangements to write to them via e-mail or the postal service, telling them in advance what documents you intend sending them and how you would like them to help you in your project. Then follow up once they've received your mail and offer any guidance they might need in providing you with the information you're seeking.

MAINTAIN CORRESPONDENCE AND RESEARCH RECORDS

Correspondence Record

It is important to keep track of those with whom you have corresponded, the reasons for writing, and whether or not you have already received an answer. A suitable Correspondence Record form is included in the downloadable files referred to in Chapter 1.

Research Calendar

As you start researching outside your own home, it will become highly advisable to keep a record of the date and details of what you searched for and where you searched for it, and the search results. Otherwise you can waste a lot of time finding you've already researched that source. This is particularly true when you start searching public records, which we'll cover in Chapter 5. We recommend that you start keeping this search record right from the beginning, using the Research Calendar to note the sources of the information as you gather it. You can then cite these sources when you enter the details into your PAF database. A Research Calendar form is included in the downloadable files referred to in Chapter 1.

TIP: RECORD KEEPING SAVES TIME LATER

Some of this record keeping may at first seem to be a bit 'over the top' and a waste of time. However, experienced genealogists all agree that it is well worth the effort and can save you many hours of unnecessary duplicated effort as you get further down the road with your genealogy project. And remember, this also helps you to validate the accuracy of your findings.

USE YOUR INDEX CARDS FOR CROSS-REFERENCING

After you complete each interview, or receive information by mail, use your index cards to make notes where information from or about one relative cross-refers to that of another relative. For example, correspondence from Linda Finn may include a lot of different information relating to a Smith ancestor that you feel should be filed in the SMITH-Correspondence sub-folder. Your index card allows you to make a note on the FINN card that there is relevant correspondence filed in the SMITH-Correspondence sub-folder. You should also include bullet-point notes of what specifically was in that correspondence.

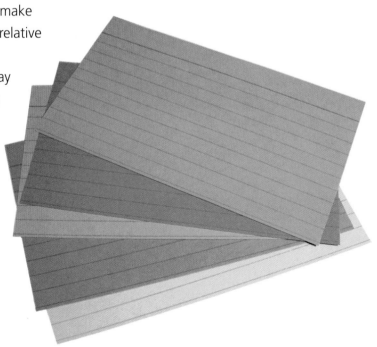

THE 'AHNENTAFEL' NUMBERING SYSTEM FOR INDIVIDUALS

Pedigree charts offer a neat graphic overview of one's line of ancestry. But they do take up a lot of pages to do that, and there are times when a more compact format is a better option. This is particularly true when a comprehensive family tree is to be published in a family history book, or when compact listings of an individual's ancestors are needed for some other purpose.

To make it possible to know who's who when such a text listing is used, it is necessary to have a numbering system in which each individual's reference number will indicate who his parents and children are in the long list of ancestors.

The most popular ancestral numbering list system is known as an *Ahnentafel* (pronounced **ah**-nin-*tah*-ful). This is a German word that literally means ancestor *(ahnen)* table *(tafel)* or ancestor list. Every budding genealogist needs to know and understand the Ahnentafel and how its numbering system works. Not only does the Ahnentafel indicate who one's own parents are in the list, but the numbering system continues to reflect this information through every ancestral generation. In this way one can see by the individual's reference number just how they relate to others in the list, both backwards and forwards in generation.

An Ahnentafel not only lists the full names of each individual, but also the date and place of birth, marriage and death, where these details are known. Once you're accustomed to reading an Ahnentafel, you'll find it easy to move up and down the list and know the relationships of the various people in the list. And the numbering system is the key to understanding Ahnentafels and being able to use them for your own ancestry.

The Ahnentafel numbering system

1   In PAF, follow the procedure on page 30, under the heading PRINTING REPORTS, to print a pedigree chart, with yourself in the primary position.
2   Note that in the pedigree chart your father's name appears in position number 2; this is double your own number (1 x 2 = 2).
3   Note that your mother's reference number 3 is your number doubled, plus one, i.e. (1 x 2) + 1 = 3; this is also your father's number plus 1.

The above example shows how the Ahnentafel numbering system works:
• The individual's number (1) multiplied by 2 gives his/her father's number (2).
• Add 1 to that father's number (2), and you get the mother's number (3).

In the Ahnentafel system, except for the first individual whose ancestral line you are recording, every male has an even number (2, 4, 6, 8, etc.) and every female has an odd number (3, 5, 7, 9, etc.). Also the female whose odd number is one more than the male's number is that male's wife. For further clarification, study the following chart carefully, then read the notes that follow it. It is a mock-up of a pedigree chart of the kind that you can print out from PAF, via File > Print Reports. You'll see that the PAF pedigree chart has the same numbering system as the following mock-up.

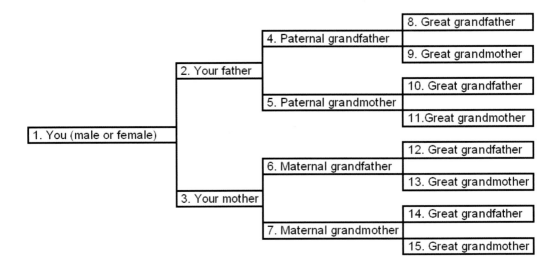

Carefully observe the reference numbers in the chart above. You will notice that every person listed has a number; and there is a mathematical relationship between parents and children.

• The number of a father is always double that of his child's.
• The number of the mother is always double that of her child's, plus one.
• The number of a child is always one-half that of a parent (ignoring any remainder).

In the above example, the father of person number 6 is number 12 (the father is double the child's number). The mother of 6 is 13 (the mother is double the child's number, plus one). The child of 12 and 13 is 6 (the child is always one-half the parent's number, ignoring remainders).

When written in the Ahnentafel format, the chart above would be listed as shown here. Except for the starting individual, the males all have even numbers. The females all have odd numbers, as explained, and the wife of a male has her husband's number, plus one. Notice that the numbers in the Ahnentafel are exactly the same as in the pedigree chart. The rules remain the same:

father = 2 x child
mother = 2 x child, +1
child   = one-half of parent, and so on.

Ahnentafel Chart for Mr Gavin Stannard HOOLE

First Generation

1. **Mr Gavin Stannard HOOLE** was born on 17 Nov 1940 in Port Elizabeth, Eastern Cape, South Africa. He was christened in Port Elizabeth, Eastern Cape, South Africa.

Gavin married **Carole Elizabeth VORSTER** daughter of Daniel Johannes VORSTER and Mrs Marie VORSTER on 20 Jun 1967. Carole was born on 16 May 1945 in Elliot, Eastern Cape, South Africa.

Second Generation

2. **Graham Fraser HOOLE** was born on 26 Apr 1906 in Cradock, Eastern Cape, South Africa. He died on 13 Apr 1981 in Port Elizabeth, Eastern Cape, South Africa. He married Phyllis Victoria STANNARD.

3. **Phyllis Victoria STANNARD** was born on 24 Aug 1908 in Port Elizabeth, Eastern Cape, South Africa. She died on 17 Jan 1991 in Port Elizabeth, Eastern Cape, South Africa.

Third Generation

4. **Oliver Percival Porter HOOLE (II)** was born on 22 Aug 1877 in Oudtshoorn, Western Cape, South Africa. He died on 2 Jun 1961 in Zuider Paarl, Western Cape, South Africa. He married Lilian Fraser ROW.

5. **Lilian Fraser ROW** was born in 1878. She died about 1970.

6. **Arthur Harry STANNARD** .Arthur married Mrs Arthur Harry STANNARD.

7. **Mrs Arthur Harry STANNARD** .

Fourth Generation

8. **Oliver Percival Porter HOOLE (I)** was born on 15 Jan 1850 in Grahamstown, Eastern Cape, South Africa. He died on 16 Aug 1929 in 'Oakvilla', Kirkwood, Eastern Cape, South Africa . He married Lydia TAUTE in 1872.

9. **Lydia TAUTE** was born on 1 Mar 1850 in Mill River, George District, Western Cape, South Africa. She died on 3 Jul 1884 in Oudtshoorn, Western Cape, South Africa.

Fifth Generation

16. **James Cottrell HOOLE** .James married Harriet Maria RHODES.

17. **Harriet Maria RHODES** .

Ahnentafel Chart generated by PAF

All modern genealogy programs can produce an Ahnentafel. You could also create an Ahnentafel by hand or by using a word processor. Whatever method you choose, an Ahnentafel is an easy method of presenting a lot of ancestral data in a compact format.

CREATING AN AHNENTAFEL IN PAF

Once you have the details of a few generations of your ancestors, you can use PAF to create your own Ahnentafel in seconds.

1 In the Menu bar, click on **File**, then on **Print Reports** (or simply press ⌨ Ctrl + P on the keyboard) to open the **Reports and Charts** dialog box.

2 Click on the **Books** tab.

3 Note the name shown as **Starting Person**. To select a different person, click on **Search**, then on either **Individual List** or **Descendancy List**, and click on the individual whose Ahnentafel you want to create.

4 Under **Type of Book**, click in the **radio button** against **Ahnentafel (Ancestry)** if it is not already selected.

5 Click on any **options** you require, as shown lower down in the box, or accept the default settings. (You may, for example, want to uncheck the option **Each generation on a new page** in order to show the Ahnentafel as one continuous report.)

6 To see a preview before printing, click on **Preview**.

7 To print the report, click on **Print**.

8 To save a copy to your Genealogy folder, click on **Print to File** (bottom right of the Reports and Charts dialog box).

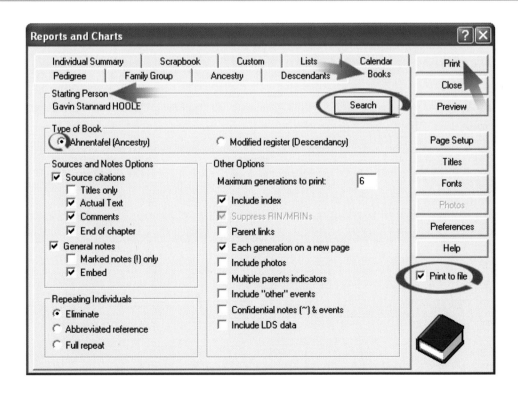

THE NEXT STEP

In the next chapter you'll start extending your ancestry search beyond your wider family circle to the Internet and other sources of public records and archives located locally and abroad.

5 Searching public records

Now it's time to broaden your research way beyond your known family circle's records. This will involve searching the Internet as well as the good old-fashioned method of visiting various archive facilities (known as 'repositories') where public records are stored and maintained for safekeeping. These repositories could include, for example, national and local government archives, church records, and the like.

Genealogists in the 21st century are most fortunate that the advent of the Internet has introduced a whole new dimension to ancestral research. The Internet is fast, convenient and very cost-effective, especially if one has a broadband connection. However, the Internet cannot always replace the old-fashioned method of making personal visits to physical resources. So this chapter will cover both approaches and will set you on the right path for this wider research in the public domain, with some tips and guidelines to help you along the way.

 STAY FOCUSED AND GOAL-ORIENTATED Avoid the temptation to leap straight in and start researching ancestors way back in time, without first having created a verified linkage from the present known generations. Also, narrow your focus and goals for each leg of your search. These two strategies could save you a lot of wasted time and avoidable frustration.

SET CLEAR SEARCH PARAMETERS AND GOALS

As your family tree extends back in time, there will be more and more branches of your ancestry that can be entered into your expanding database. This, in turn, will broaden the scope for conducting searches, and will open up many different avenues or branches you can explore. It is therefore vitally important that you take a step back and refer to your original longer-term objective as well as where the gaps are in your pedigree charts; then decide which branch you want to start researching first. If you don't have a definite sequence plan like this, with specific short-term goals, a 'shotgun approach' at research can become fragmented and frustrating.

Remember also the principle of working back one generation at a time. By working in this way you can trace your lineage more methodically and accurately, using information that establishes without doubt a definite link from one generation to the next. If you jump back several generations instead, in the hope of arriving at your longer term goals more quickly, you can end up coming to the wrong conclusions and linking the wrong ancestors to your family lineage. So, stick to the rule: work back one generation at a time (for a particular branch).

WRITE DOWN YOUR PARAMETERS AND GOALS

The choice of which branch of your ancestry to research will, of course, depend on your focus and mission. Unless you have a specific reason for doing otherwise, a good idea would be to start with one of your grandparents.

❑ From your pedigree chart, decide which ancestor you'll start researching:

_____

❑ Decide how many generations further back from that individual you wish to research in that particular branch before you start researching another branch:

_____ generations further back for this first branch of research.

❑ For that starting-point individual, determine where they lived and learn something about that area, so that you can be better equipped to know what to look for and where you might find it:

- Check whether there were any changes to boundaries, town or area names, etc., that could possibly clear up any inconsistencies or blank walls your research might lead you to.
- Check whether there were any significant historical events in or near that area that could later offer clues for your research – e.g. military battles, widespread diseases, floods, political upheavals, influential new laws that could have had an impact on the population at that time.

❑ Look at the relevant Family view screens in PAF to identify where the gaps exist in information and family details, and decide exactly what pieces of information you want to find in respect of each individual, e.g.

- their occupations;
- property owned;
- standing in the community;
- religion;
- military service;
- education and skills;
- hobbies;
- health details.

❑ With these questions clarified in your mind, write down a list of the clear goals you want to achieve with this first research venture, e.g. Where was granddad born, and when? What was *great*-granddad's name? Where and when was *he* born?

NAVIGATING THE 18TH CENTURY CALENDAR MINEFIELD

 BE CAREFUL ABOUT DATES BEFORE 1752 In 1752 a significant change was made to the Julian (Old Style) calendar system used in England and the British Colonies: the first month of the year was changed from March to January. In addition, there was a discrepancy of eleven days resulting from the late adoption by these countries of the Gregorian (New Style) calendar – some decades after it was first introduced elsewhere in the world. These factors have an impact on the interpretation of dates prior to 1752 if they were written in numerals only.

The Julian calendar, named after Julius Caesar who introduced it in 46 BC, was flawed in that, over time, it moved further and further away from the natural solar cycle. To fix this problem, in 1582 Pope Gregory XIII issued a decree to replace the flawed Julian calendar with the Gregorian calendar (named after himself). To regain synchronicity with the solar cycle, in the Gregorian calendar ten days were removed from the month of October 1582, and Leap Years were introduced to eliminate the recurrence of this synchronicity problem. A key point to be aware of in genealogical research is that a number of Protestant countries did not adopt this 'new style' Gregorian calendar until many decades later. It was adopted by Great Britain and her colonies 170 years later, while other countries, such as China, did not adopt the Gregorian calendar until the 1900's. Dates before 1752 should therefore ring an alarm bell, and the researcher needs to get the correct interpretation in order to record accurate vital details.

How to record dates from that period

To be safe, we suggest you stick with the basic rule of recording details exactly as they appear on the document you're viewing. Then do other research of various archives to see if you can pin down the date to what it most likely was, according to the country in which the event took place and was recorded. Never replace the original date with one you assume it should be; rather add your interpretation behind it in brackets or in PAF's Notes section.

There are a number of websites that can give more details on this change-over, and some that offer charts and other features that can be used to convert a Julian date to a Gregorian date, and vice versa. To find such sites, while connected to the Internet:

Go to a search engine such as Google **(http://www.google.com)** and do a search for: **Gregorian Calendar + Genealogy**, then click on the links that interest you.

TIP: ONE CLUE LEADS TO ANOTHER

Finding out roughly where your ancestor was living helps when searching for vital information, including how to interpret key dates of their life's events.

SEARCHING THE RECORDS

There are two main types of genealogical records:

- **Compiled Records:** These are records that have already been researched by others, such as biographies, family histories, or genealogies that may be on microfilm, microfiche, in books or on the FamilySearch website (see page 62).
- **Original Records:** These are records that were created at or near the time of an event, such as birth, marriage, death, or census records.

 LOOK FOR COMPILED RECORDS FIRST This could save you lots of time and effort. Finding compiled records doesn't mean there won't be mistakes or wrong information. But, you might be surprised at what research may already have been done on your family lines. Once you've exhausted your search for compiled records, it's then time to start searching for original records.

KINDS OF RECORDS TO LOOK FOR

• Census	You need to know when and where your ancestor was living in order to find the correct census. Census records can be found in National Archives as well as online. (If you don't know where they lived, some of the online censuses do have a 'search' facility.)
• Churches	Churches or parishes – the original places that kept track of local families in the birthplace or home town of your ancestor – are where you'd find records of baptisms, marriages and burials.
• Emigration and immigration	Your ancestors at one time or another may have emigrated from their native soil to another country. In reverse, they may have immigrated into a new country from their native home. National Archives hold immigration and emigration records of such moves.
• Land and property	Property deeds, found in local court houses, often give hints of what kind of wealth or lack of wealth an ancestor might have had, as well as physical addresses and dates of property ownership.
• Military	Military records can be found in National Archives of the country where an ancestor served. They can provide additional information and act as a source of some vital details.
• Naturalization and citizenship	Found in state, county or local court records, these files can also provide some revealing details about an ancestor, such as a name change and confirmation of key dates perhaps not found in other records.
• Probate/Wills/Estates	Probate: proving a will is genuine. Will: a legal document of how a person wants their property to be distributed after their death. Estate: The sum total of all of a person's property at death. These documents can be found in both national and local archives, and can give insights into personal relationships as well as an ancestor's property and financial standing.
• Vital statistics records	Birth, death, marriage and divorce certificates are maintained by local or civil authorities. (Marriage details are also kept in church records.)
• Old newspapers	Visit the library in the city where an ancestor once lived and view microfilm/microfiche of newspapers published at the time an ancestor may have resided in that area.
• Cemeteries	Search for familiar names on tombstones. Dates of birth and death are usually recorded on the tombstone. Visit the offices located in most cemeteries and ask to view their records to find the location of a tombstone of interest more easily.
• Passenger lists	These are lists of the names and dates of arrival of immigrants into another country's port. The name of the ship is often included too. Passenger lists can be found on the Internet at National Archives websites as well as specific seaports' websites. (e.g. http://www.ellisisland.org)
• Institutions	The impact of poverty and life in a workhouse may be documented in official records stored in a local records office or in a historical society. Institutions can include prisons, hospitals, asylums, schools, orphanages and any charitable organizations.

MICROFORM IMAGES

Microforms are films containing document images that are typically 25 times smaller than the original size. They may come as either positives or negatives, the latter giving a clearer visual image on a special reader, or when printed. The two formats are microfilm which comes in a reel, and microfiche, a flat sheet format.

Microfiche sheet behind, and Microfilm roll in front

OBTAINING CERTIFIED EXTRACTS FROM ORIGINAL DOCUMENTS

If original certificates are lost forever, the next best step would be to contact the Registrar General in the district where you suspect the incident – a birth, for example – was recorded. For a small fee you can obtain a certified copy of the birth certificate. This information would be extracted from register entries held in the custody of the Superintendent Registrar and would definitely be considered a primary source (see the following illustrations).

An original Certificate of Marriage, 31 Dec 1914

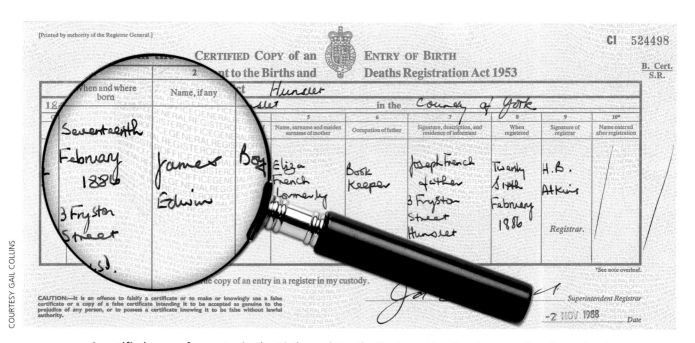

A certified copy of an entry in the Births and Deaths Register, Hunslet, County of York, England

TIP: CHECK VARIATIONS OF SURNAMES

Surnames may have changed over time, either intentionally or owing to transcription errors, so be sure to check other variations of surnames you're looking for. Your ancestor may have always spelt or signed his or her name a certain way, but those who actually recorded their name – census takers, county clerks and tax collectors – may have spelt it in various other ways. Many an immigrant could not spell (in English) her or his name. So when they gave their name to county clerks, enumerators, etc., that person wrote the name as it sounded to him.

TIP: WATCH OUT FOR NAME CHANGES

You can be searching your roots and not be aware that your grandfather was adopted and that his surname was officially and legally changed, and a new birth certificate issued with his 'new' family's name. Be aware that unless you uncover that he had been adopted, you could be researching who you think are his blood relatives when in fact they're not. So keep an eye open for any clues that could indicate that an adoption may have occurred.

 NEVER ASSUME Many family historians assume they've found the correct relative and make the mistake of tracing the family history of someone totally unrelated to them. Get into the habit of cross-checking to verify details.

USING THE INTERNET

Most beginner genealogists would prefer to start off their wider search by using the Internet from the comfort of their own home (or at a local Internet-connected library or Internet Café). We support this approach because these days you can find a wealth of information in this way. It makes sense first to see what you can gather from the World Wide Web before leaving your base at home to explore libraries and other archive and information sources, some of which could be quite some distance away.

Once your initial Internet research has been done, you can then go out and do the field work and come back home to consolidate the information gathered via both methods. You will most likely need to surf the Internet again as you find additional information from your field trips, and vice versa. So, the Internet and physical visits really go hand in hand in a two-prong approach to your research.

TIP: NEED AN INTERNET CONNECTION?

If you're away from home and need a computer or Internet connection, visit a library (usually free) or an Internet café (at a cost).

Immigration Identification Cards found in the author's parents' home after their deaths

This Travelling Tickets folder containing Immigration Identification Cards confirm that 30 Jun 1929 was the date her father immigrated to Quebec, Canada, aboard the Laurentic. Armed with this arrival date, the author used the Internet to search the National Archives of Canada and was able to obtain further detailed information on her father (see screenshot on the right). This demonstrates how one piece of information can lead to further discoveries, often opening new doors after all others have been closed.

Results of the Internet search

By doing the Internet search later, the author found that the information on the Immigration Identification Card (left) matched that of the Immigration Records (1925-1935) found on the Internet. In addition, the Internet archive showed that her father had arrived from England into the Port of Quebec City in Quebec, Canada. The Microfilm reel number is also recorded, so she was even able to take her research a step further and obtain copies of the original immigration records. Chapter 5 shows you how to do Internet searches specifically in respect of ancestry.

USING THE LDS FAMILY HISTORY LIBRARY, SALT LAKE CITY

Considered to be the mother of all genealogical resources, the Family History Library in Salt Lake City, Utah, USA, is owned and operated by the Corporation of the President of The Church of Jesus Christ of Latter-day Saints. It provides access not only to scores of genealogical records and computerized indexes but also to a wealth of helpful information for beginners as well as professionals. It features more than 957 million names in its searchable databases. The physical and website addresses are:

The Family History Library of the Church of Jesus
    Christ of Latter-day Saints (Mormons)
35 North West Temple Street
Salt Lake City, UT 84150-3400
Website: **http://www.familysearch.org**

The quickest way to access their records is via the FamilySearch website above.

Family History Library
Salt Lake City, Utah

BENEFITING FROM ONLINE COLLABORATION

In genealogy, two researchers working hand in hand can accomplish much more than one person working entirely on their own. And if this process is expanded into a group situation, even greater results can be achieved. Here's a website that will help you enjoy the benefits of collaboration via the Internet.

RootsWeb.com – supported by Ancestry.com **http://www.rootsweb.com**

This is a site dedicated to connecting genealogists so that they can help one another expand their family tree databases by exchanging their research findings. It's a good place to start expanding your own genealogy expertise and also your own family tree.

One of the primary tools on RootsWeb.com that online genealogists make use of, in order to contact each other and share information, is the RootsWeb Surname List (RSL). This is a registry of over a million surname entries that have been submitted by approximately 300,000 online genealogists. Associated with each surname are dates, locations, and information about how to contact the person who submitted the surname.

Here are some of the things you can do at RootsWeb.com:

• Submit your own surname to RootsWeb RSL to make it easy for others to find you.

• Use the mailing list and message boards to ask for help and give help to others, and to receive information of interest to you.

• Search the ancestries of others for missing ancestor details needed for your own family tree.

• Upload your own family tree so that others with common ancestors can access your ancestry to fill in the gaps in their own family tree.

• Build your very own genealogy website at RootsWeb.com (not as difficult as it sounds), and request free Web space to host it.

• Link your RootsWeb.com website to the relevant surname and/or location clusters to gain greater exposure and build your circle of collaborating genealogists.

EXCHANGING PAF FILES IN GEDCOM FILE FORMAT

The best way to share your PAF family tree files with others is by making your file available in a format that other genealogy computer programs can use. The GEDCOM format serves this purpose. With GEDCOM you can e-mail your information, include the file on your website or submit it to a genealogy site so that others can access it from the site's database. You can recognize a GEDCOM file by the extension **.ged** at the end of the file name. If you use PAF to generate a Web page, it automatically provides a GEDCOM file link on your Web page so that others can download your ancestry in that way. For further details about GEDCOM files, refer to the PAF User's Guide or Lessons.

> **!** **INFORMATION ON THE INTERNET IS NOT INFALLIBLE** The Internet is only as accurate as the people who provide the data. It is a very useful method of obtaining information, but the usual rules of cross-checking and verifying what you find via the Internet are still very important, perhaps even more so.

SEARCHING CENSUS RECORDS

A census – an official periodic count, on a specific date, of the population of a particular nation – is usually conducted every ten years in most industrialized countries. Some nations, such as Canada, hold an interim census at the five-year interval between the decennial census, often on a random sample basis. Today, some countries are able to complete their census online. The results are documented in census records held by the government.

When searching census records for a relative that you feel you know for certain lived in such-and-such a place during a given census year, be aware that boundaries do change over time. During the ten year period between each census, borders may have changed for a province or even an entire country. When searching census records, first check whether there have been any boundary changes since the last census. If so, check for your ancestor in the census of both counties/countries – the 'old' one and the 'new' one – to increase your chances of finding them.

No. of Schedule	ROAD, STREET, etc., and No. or NAME of HOUSE	HOUSES In-hab ited	HOUSES Unin hab ited of Bldg	NAME and Surname of each Person	RELATION to Head of Family	CON-DITION	AGE of Males	AGE of Females	Rank, Profession, or OCCUPATION	WHERE BORN	Whether 1. Deaf-and-Dumb 2. Blind 3. Imbecile or Idiot 4. Lunatic
36	Giles Rd.	1		James LEEDER	Head	M	47		Brickmaker	Norfolk, Gunthorpe	
				Maria do	Wife	M		51/58?	–	Suffolk, Brandon	
				James T. do	Son	S	26		Agricultural Labourer	Norfolk, Swanton Novers	
				Robert do	do	S	24		Shepherd	do do	
				Alvina do	Daur	S		21	Washer woman	do do	
				Jessie do	Son	S	?		Agricultural labourer	do do	
				Walter do	do	S	16		do do	do do	
				Herbert T. do	Son	–	14		do do	do do	
37	do	1		James S. LEEDER	Head	M	62		Agricultural Labourer	do do	
				Mary do	Wife	M		58	–	Suffolk, Brandon	
				Priscilla do	Daur	S		23?	–	Norfolk, Swanton Novers	
				Hilda? M. do	Grand Daur	–		2?	–	Do Do	
38	do	1		John BULLOCK	Head	M	24		Agricultural Labourer	Do Do	
				Adelaide do	Wife	M		23	–	Do Do	
39		1		George DUCKER	Head	M	34		Do Do	Do Do	
				Mary do	Wife	M		36	–	Do Do	
				Mable do	Daur	–		6	Scholar	Do Do	
				Elizabeth do	do	–		4	Do	Do Do	
				George do	Son	–	2?		–	Do Do	
				Robert do	do	–	? mos?		–	Do Do	
				Robert BULLEN	Lodger	S	22		Agricultural Labourer	Do Do	
40	Do	1		John MUSSETT	Head	Widr	83		Living on his own means	Do Do	–
	Total of Houses...					Total of Males and Females...					

The undermentioned Houses are situate within the Boundaries of the — Page 6

Civil Parish (or Township) of — Swanton Novers
City or Municipal Borough of
Municipal Ward of
Parliamentary Borough of — North Norfolk
Town of
Village or Hamlet, etc., of — Swanton Novers
Local Board or (Improvement Commissioners District) of — Walsingham
Ecclesiastical District of

COURTESY JUANITA HADWIN

Census extract

A handwritten copy of an extract from an 1891 Census (Norfolk, England) – transcribed from microfiche of the original census record that was obtained from a local LDS Family History Centre

Availability of census records

For reasons of privacy, there is a moratorium on the release to the public of census details, ranging from 70 to 100 years, for example.

	Privacy Period	Year of First Useful Census Records	Last Released Census
U.S.A.	72 years	1790	1930
U.K.	100 years	1841 (no 1941 census due to war)	1901
Canada	92 years	1871	1911

Where to find some census record abstracts (blank forms for specific census years):

USA: http://www.ancestry.com/trees/charts/census.aspx

UK: http://www.ancestry.com/trees/charts/ukcensus.aspx

CANADA: http://www.ancestry.com/trees/charts/canadacensus.aspx

OPTIMIZING YOUR INTERNET SEARCHES

- Search engines are not case sensitive. Genealogy, genealogy, GeNeAlOgY, etc., will all bring up the same results.
- Search engines exclude common words, such as *and, the,* etc.
- **Census Records England** brings up millions of possibilities, whereas typing quotes before and after the search phrase brings up more precise hits, e.g. **'Census Records England'**.
- **Census Records** brings up census information for all countries.
- **Census Records -U.S. -Canada** (minus signs) eliminates the country or countries you know don't pertain to your search. If the results show areas or States you don't want included, add them to the search criteria with a minus sign, and try again.
- If you want all census records for a specific country, add the country's name with a (+) plus sign in front of it, e.g. **Census Records +Ireland**.
- If you know the specific census year you want to search, add the year with a (+) plus sign in front of it, e.g. **Census Records +1766**.

See Chapter 6 for some good websites that are worth a visit.

TIP: CLICK ON THE WEBSITE LINKS VIA OUR WEBSITE

All the website addresses mentioned in this book, plus more, are given as click-on links at our own genealogy website. To go straight to a site, simply click on its link. Also, genealogists are invited to share useful sites with others by visiting our genealogy forum which can be accessed via our main site. http://www.ReallyEasyComputerBooks.com

LDS Family History Centres Worldwide
(more than 4,000 branches worldwide)

These centres are branch facilities of the Family History Library in Salt Lake City, Utah. They have been set up to provide access to most of the microfilms and microfiche in the actual Family History Library in Utah, to help people identify their ancestors without having to travel to Utah to do it. You do not have to be a member of the LDS Church to make use of their massive database: everyone is welcome.

How to find a Family History Centre near you

Via the Internet:
1   Connect to the Internet and visit the website at **http://www.familysearch.org**
2   Click on the **Library** tab, then on the **Family History Centres** link.
3   In the window that opens, click on the ⌄ **down** arrow to select your country.
4   Type your province/county/city into the appropriate boxes. (If you enter only the State/Province, or only the Country, the search results will list all centres in that broader area you specified.)
5   Click on **Search**.

Via your telephone directory:
1   Look up the name **Church of Jesus Christ of Latter Day Saints**.
2   Look down the list of entries to find **Family History Centre**. (If a centre is not listed, call the main phone number in the list.)

PREPARE FOR YOUR FIELD TRIP

At some point you will probably need to go to a library, a branch of the National Archives, or some other location to do some research on your family. To make the most of your visit, make sure you're well prepared when you get there. If possible, decide on a day when you'll have several hours free, and start early. There's nothing more frustrating than finding some great information right before you have to leave to come home.

Call beforehand to get some details:

- ❑ the days and hours they are open
- ❑ whether they're open to the general public
- ❑ any fees that must be paid, and what they are – e.g. entrance, parking, photocopying
- ❑ directions and parking information
- ❑ whether there are any access requirements (identification, photo ID, etc.)
- ❑ whether any proof of relationship is required for accessing old ancestral documents
- ❑ any restrictions that apply – e.g. the use of pens, cameras, laptop computers, cell phones
- ❑ whether there are any public refreshment facilities on site, or nearby (restaurant, coffee shop, vending machine)

Pack a research case or bag:

- ❑ black ink pens and pencils (some places do not allow the use of pens), with spares
- ❑ paper to write on, file folders
- ❑ magnifying glass
- ❑ printouts of relevant genealogy charts and forms and PAF reports, e.g. family group, pedigree chart(s), source citations, blank census forms
- ❑ your list of questions you want answered by your research
- ❑ photocopies (keep your originals safely at home) of the information you already have on the branch(es) of the family you're planning to research (When you find something new, you can check your existing facts to see if the information matches up.)
- ❑ enough small change to pay all the necessary fees, as well as buy refreshments if necessary

NATIONAL GOVERNMENT REPOSITORIES

Many countries maintain archives of all documents that are directly related to the daily operation of the national government and its branches, agencies or ministries.

Chapter 6 includes the physical addresses and website addresses of the national repositories of several countries. Contact details of the archives office are given on each website.

If your country is not included in our list, you can use the Internet to look for your own country's national repository. In a search engine such as Google, for example, do a search for the words National Archives +(Your Country) – e.g. **National Archives +Italy**. That should open a page of links to your national archives website and probably to branch offices and related Web pages as well.

COURTESY NATALIE DRACHE

Name change / death certificates can be found in local government vital statistics offices or can be requested on the Internet.

SEARCHING AT CEMETERIES

Visit old churches and cemeteries in the area(s) where your ancestors died and ask permission to see old church records. Search for familiar names on tombstones; they may help to confirm dates of birth, death and in some instances, names of spouses and/or children.

COURTESY PAULINE AND JAMES SIMPSON

The inscription on this tombstone – 'In loving memory of John Ducker who departed this life February 16th 1888 aged 68 years' – confirmed the birth and death dates of an ancestor.

How one clue leads to another. OLBERG: This gravestone states the age of an ancestor and the date of death. These details, in turn, confirmed the date of birth. DUCKER: This contributor knew that her ancestor, although with the British Navy, was buried somewhere in Malta – but why and where? She searched for and found his naval records in England, which confirmed the stories she had heard as a child: that due to an accident, he died while in port in Malta. His records cited the name of the cemetery in Malta where he was buried, and the gravestone was found by the contributor.

OLBERG: COURTESY NATALIE DRACHE
DUCKER: COURTESY JUANITA HADWIN

Tips for a cemetery visit

- **Take clippers to clear invasive undergrowth:** Clippers will come in handy if you need to cut away overgrown grass or thicket that is obscuring the grave or the stone.

- **Take a mirror to enhance inscription readability:** If the stone is in shadow, a mirror can help to brighten the carvings for better visibility. On a sunny day, it is useful to face towards the sun while looking at the stone. This old Boy Scout tracking technique helps to make the shadows of the carvings more clearly visible.

- **Take some water and a nylon brush:** If the stone is covered in grit and grime, a bottle of water and a gentle wash down with a nylon brush can improve readability considerably.

- **Sketch a grave location map:** It's a good idea to draw a rough sketch of the layout and to pinpoint certain landmarks to help you in the event of a repeat visit, and also as a guide for anyone following in your footsteps later. A useful Cemetery Record mapping form can be downloaded free at: **http://www.cs.williams.edu/~bailey/genealogy/Cemetery1.pdf**, with page 2 available at **http://www.cs.williams.edu/~bailey/genealogy/Cemetery2.pdf.** Photographs of a large area around the grave will also be useful for finding the location in future.

- **Record details accurately:** Write down the details exactly as they are shown on the stone and make a sketch of any symbols or insignia shown too; these could suggest that the ancestor belonged to a particular organization or religion. Better still, take a camera and photograph the stone and its detailed inscriptions.

- **Check behind the stone too:** Check for any inscriptions on the back of tombstones too – not always an obvious place to look, but sometimes a source of important details.

- **Note any relationships mentioned:** Note down any other names mentioned on the stone – family and other relationships – and look around at nearby graves as well, in case family members or close friends may be buried alongside the ancestor you are researching.

GETTING CLOSER TO THE GOAL

This brings us to the end of this never-ending journey called genealogy. As you keep finding more and more details about your ancestors, and continue updating your family tree and family history, over time you'll move closer and closer to your original goals. These may be publishing your own family history on the World Wide Web or in a book, or creating a family tree chart showing the many generations of your ancestors, culminating in your own family unit of the present day.

We hope this beginner's book has helped you to get started and make some good progress with this very interesting and increasingly popular pastime of genealogy.

All the best!

COURTESY GAVIN HOOLE

Family history and family tree books – the results of years of dedicated genealogy research by the books' authors

Web page generated easily and automatically with PAF, via Tools, Create Web Page...

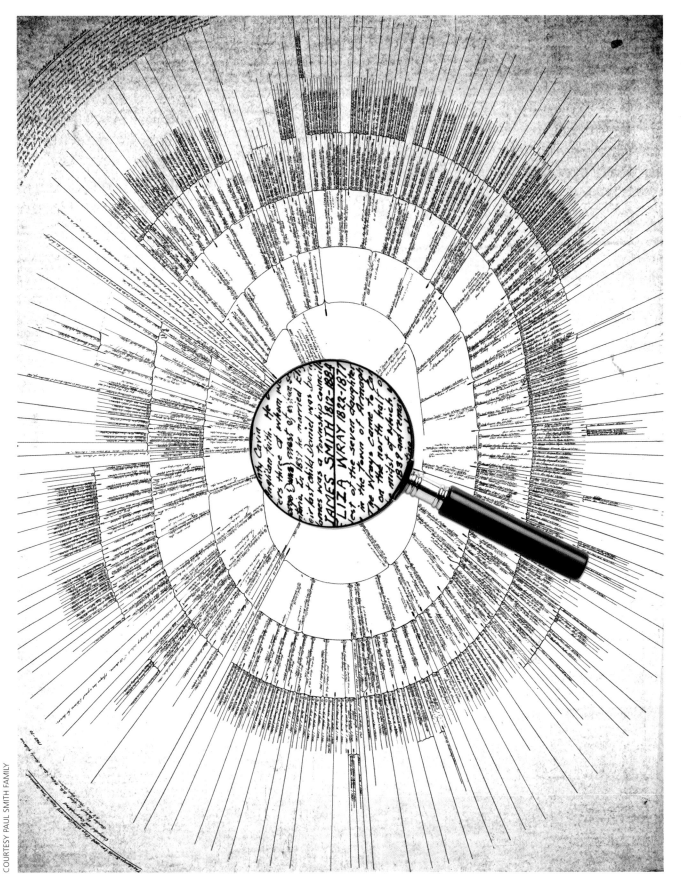

The rewarding culmination of many hours of research and documenting, done over many years: Smith family wheel spanning seven generations, beginning with the union of James Smith, born 1812, and Eliza Wray, born 1822

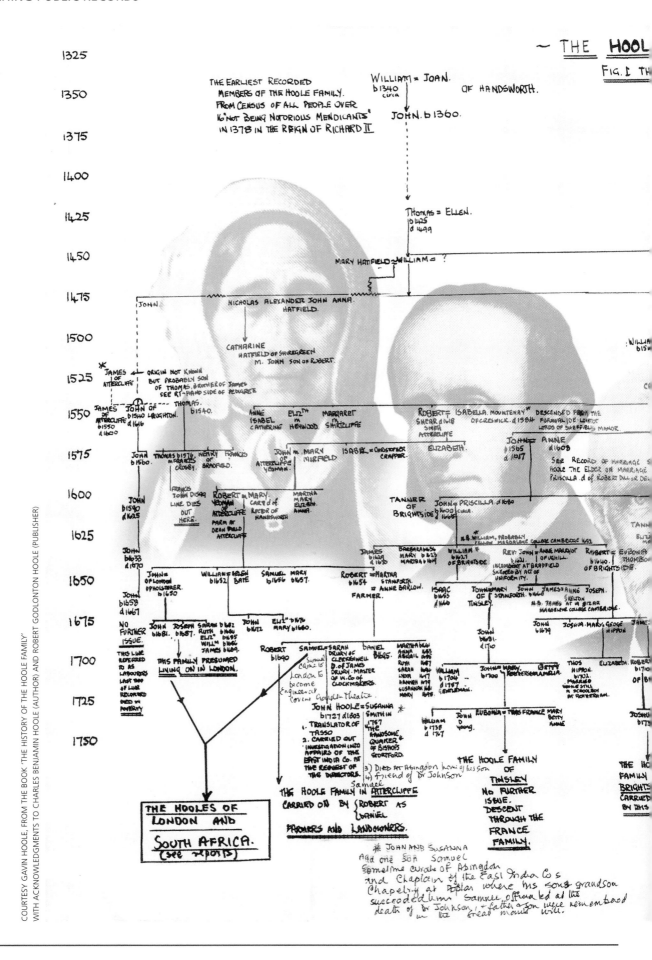

COURTESY GAVIN HOOLE, FROM THE BOOK 'THE HISTORY OF THE HOOLE FAMILY'
WITH ACKNOWLEDGMENTS TO CHARLES BENJAMIN HOOLE (AUTHOR) AND ROBERT GODLONTON HOOLE (PUBLISHER)

SHEFFIELD —

N EARLY TIMES 1325 to 1750

THOMAS b 1450

THOMAS. b 1475.

ROBERT = MARGARET OF WINCOBANK.
d 1546   LIVED AT
see WILL "BRIKFORD"
IN TEXT.

JOHN = CATHARINE HATFIELD
d. of NICHOLAS HATFIELD.

ELIZABETH JANET.

THOMAS. PROBABLE FATHER OF JAMES OF ATTERCLIFFE SEE # ON LEAF OF PEDIGREE USE OF PATERNAL NAME THOMAS IS THE ONLY INDICATION (AND JAMES)

JAMES = ISABEL.
b 1509
d 1574
SHEARSMITH

ISABEL b 1520
ELIZ B M.

JOHN = HIS COUSIN CATHERINE HOOLE
b 1521   d. of WILLIAM / ALICE.

WILLIAM ELIZ TH JANE.

WILLIAM = ELIZABETH HOBSON.

20th AUGUST 1620 WM HOOLE OF CROOKES GRANTS TO HIS SON CHARLES A MESSUAGE IN CROOKES TOWNGATE

WILLIAM = ANNE WEBSTER
b 1567
d 1639

20TH JULY 1616 CHARLES HOOLE OF SHEFFIELD CORVISOR GRANTS TO JOHN HOOLE, A TANNER AND HIS BROTHER, A MESSUAGE IN CROOKES IN OCCUPATION.

CHARLES = ANNE OR AGNES CRESWICK
b 1571   2) MARY ? AT WAKEFIELD
d 1629   * IT IS BELIEVED THAT A ROBERT
CORVISOR (SHOEMAKER) HOOLE ALREADY LIVED IN
OF UPPERTHORPE WAKEFIELD WITH SON JOHN
AND WAKEFIELD. b 1613
SHEFFIELD

20TH JUNE 1603 THOS SCARGILL OF SHEFFIELD GRANTS TO WM HOOLE OF GEORGE AND JOHN HOOLE A TANNER A COTTING CALLED WILLIAMS CLOSE AND A WELL SHEFFIELD WELL

ANNE b 1610 MARGARET b 1636 ALICE b 1632

ROBERT b 1618 d 1636

JAMES = HELEN FISHER b 1616 2) MARGARET LINLEY

ROBERT AND GEORGE OF WAKEFIELD → HOOLE FAMILY OF WAKEFIELD

JAMES = MARY FRANCIS b 1641 FREEMAN CUTLER 1636 APPRENTICED BY HIS FATHER TO ED. CRESWICK

CHARLES M.A b 1609 d 1677 EDUCATED WAKEFIELD G. ST LINCOLN COLLEGE OXFORD. BECAME SCHOOLMASTER EDUCATION AUTHORITY ONE-TIME MASTER ROTHERHAM G.S.

WILLIAM = ELIZAB TH b 1606

JANE ROSA AGNES MARY.

JOHN b 1615 OF CROOKES d 1670 TANNER

12TH MARCH 1654 JOHN HOOLE OF CROOKES FOR £67 MORTGAGE 20 ACRES ADJOINING WELL A COMMON CELLAR BELL 1694 BON SALE IN THE MONTH

WILLIAM CIRCA 1650

JOHN = LYDIA SMITH

JAMES MARY AGNES ROBERT 1644 1649 JOSEPH 1643 WILLIAM 1640

ANNE SARAH.

JAMES = MARGARET 1) KIRK b 1637 2) JOAN JONES

ANNE ELIZABETH.

WILLIAM b 1635 d 1677

JOHN b 1638 d 1641

ELIZABETH = JAMES SPOONER NO ISSUE

JOHN = ALICE

MARGARET ALICE. NO MALE b 1632. 1658

JAMES b 1663 JUDITH ASHE MASTER CUTLER 2) BRIDGET 1708 MELDON

SAMUEL b 1664

WILLIAM b 1662.

MARY ANNA.

WILLIAM = SARAH ELLIOTT b 1692

JOHN = SARAH NEWTON

ROBERT. MARY = WM b 1693 BRADSHAW

ELIZ = J MACHON LYDIA = THOS NEWTON

JAMES = MARY ANNE PLATT YEOMAN OF CROOKES

THE ORIGINS OF HOOLES OF SHEFFIELD WHO BECAME CUTLERS AND BUTTON MAKERS

SARAH b 1698

JOSEPH b 1692

RUTH. b 1695

WILLIAM = MARTHA b 1711. ELLIOTT PREMIER CUTLER d. of COL.

THOMAS NO ISSUE

GEORGE = HANNAH. GRINDER AND CUTLER.

ENSIGN OF ROYAL BODYGUARD OF GEORGE II AT HIS DEATH IN HANOVER.

IT IS NOT KNOWN WHETHER THIS BRANCH CONTINUED IN SHEFFIELD OR WAKEFIELD.

HENRY = ALICE b 1735 LON. d 1804

THOMAS LON. d 1806

JOHN = RACHEL. b 1755.

JOHN b 1776

JOHN b 1779

THE HOOLE FAMILY OF CROOKES. SEE FIG. III FOR COMPLETE PEDIGREE

THE DESCENDENTS OF C.B HOOLE OF BASLOW. SEE FIG IV FOR COMPLETE PEDIGREE.

THE HOOLE FAMILY OF HALLAMGATE SEE FIG V FOR COMPLETE PEDIGREE.

NOTES DEC 3RD 1961.

1) THESE PEDIGREES HAVE BEEN ASSEMBLED FROM CONTEMPORARY AND OTHER RECORDS FROM THE SHEFFIELD REFERENCE LIBRARY

2) COPIES OF MOST OF THESE ARE ON MICRO-FILM. THE ORIGINALS ARE IN THE BRITISH MUSEUM.

3) REGISTERS OF BIRTHS DEATHS & MARRIAGES HAVE ONLY BEEN USED TO VERIFY THE PEDIGREES USED. AS EACH BRANCH BECAME UNRECORDED, THE PEDIGREE WAS LEFT AT THAT POINT TO AVOID THE DANGERS OF INACCURACY AND GUESSWORK.

4) NUMEROUS HISTORICAL REFERENCES FROM THE SAME SOURCE HAVE BEEN USED TO CHECK THE PEDIGREES IN MANY INSTANCES

FIG VI. THE LOWSLEY-WILLIAMS FAMILY OF CHAVENAGE TETBURY GLOS

Family tree going back to the 1300's

6 Some useful resources

NATIONAL LIBRARIES AND ARCHIVES

THE NATIONAL ARCHIVES (U.K.)
Kew, Richmond
Surrey TW9 4DU, England
http://nationalarchives.gov.uk

THE NATIONAL ARCHIVES OF IRELAND
Bishop Street
Dublin 8, Ireland
http://www.nationalarchives.ie

THE NATIONAL LIBRARY OF WALES
Penglais Hill
Aberystwyth, Ceredigion
Wales SY23 3BU, UK
http://llgc.org.uk

LIBRARY AND ARCHIVES CANADA
395 Wellington Street
Ottawa, ON K1A 0N4, Canada
http://www.collectionscanada.ca

THE NATIONAL ARCHIVES OF AUSTRALIA
Queen Victoria Terrace, Parkes
ACT 2600, Australia
http://www.naa.gov.au

NATIONAL ARCHIVES AND RECORDS SERVICE (NARS) OF SOUTH AFRICA
The National Archivist
24 Hamilton Street
Arcadia, Pretoria 0001, South Africa
http://www.national.archives.gov.za

ARCHIVES NEW ZEALAND
10 Mulgrave Street, Thorndon,
Wellington, New Zealand
http://www.archives.govt.nz

THE NATIONAL ARCHIVES OF SCOTLAND
2 Princes Street, Edinburgh
EH1 3YY, Scotland
http://www.nas.gov.uk

THE NATIONAL ARCHIVES AND RECORDS ADMINISTRATION (U.S.)
700 Pennsylvania Avenue, NW,
Washington, D.C. 20408, USA
http://www.archives.gov

OTHER INTERNET RESOURCES

Cyndi's List http://www.cyndislist.com This site provides links to well over 150,000 genealogical websites around the world. It is particularly strong for the USA and can be a little overwhelming, so handle with care.

Naturalization Records http://naturalizationrecords.com This site is devoted to naturalization and immigration records.

Census Records http://allcensusrecords.com This site describes itself as the One-Stop Site for links to USA Census Records, Canadian Census Records, English Census Records, Census Indexes & Images, Census Transcriptions, Blank Census Forms, City Directories, Tax & Assessment Lists, Voters Registrations, Veterans Census, Questions on Census Records.

FamilyRecords.gov.uk http://www.familyrecords.gov.uk This site is a joint effort by government departments and public sector bodies and provides a treasure-trove of information in one Web location. Together these bodies hold much of the primary source material that can be hard to find if you don't know which institution holds the records you need.

Convicts to Australia http://www.convictcentral.com This website is a guide to researching convict ancestors. While the vast majority of the convicts to Australia were English (70%), Irish (24%) or Scottish (5%), the convict population had a multicultural flavour and included convicts from such places as India, Canada, New Zealand and Hong Kong. The site also includes list of slaves from the Caribbean.

British Passenger Lists, 1878 – 1960 http://www.passengerlists.co.uk This site contains the names and details of 100,000 passengers – men, women, children – who travelled in or out of any British port between 1878 and 1960, including passengers travelling worldwide via the United Kingdom.

findmypast.com http://www.findmypast.com This site has a massive database of British records that include births, deaths, marriages, (including those at sea), as well as adoption, military records, census records, passenger lists, passport applications, parish registers, wills and probate, occupations, WW1, WW2 and the Boer War deaths, and even a search for tracing living relatives.

Ancestors on Board (developed by findmypast.com) http://www.ancestorsonboard.com
Here you can search over 30 million records of individuals or groups of people leaving for destinations including Australia, Canada, India, New Zealand, South Africa and the USA, featuring ports such as Boston, Philadelphia and New York. Images of the passenger lists are available to download, view, save and print. The site now includes Outward Passenger Lists for long-distance voyages leaving the British Isles from 1960 right back to 1890.

British 1820 Settlers to South Africa **http://www.1820settlers.com** This website, with totally free access and use by researchers and contributors alike, is dedicated to the British Settlers who arrived in South Africa in 1820, and to their descendants and researchers. The information has been supplied or posted by the members of this website.

Ancestors at Rest (US, Canada, England) **http://ancestorsatrest.com** At this site you can search for your ancestors through death records. It offers free databases such as coffin plates, death cards, funeral cards, wills, church records, family Bibles, cenotaphs and tombstone inscriptions.

Ancestry.com **http://www.ancestry.com** Becoming a member on Ancestry.com is quite expensive but this site does offer a lot of useful information.

FreeBMD **http://freebmd.rootsweb.com/cgi/search.pl** FreeBMD is an ongoing project, the aim of which is to transcribe the Civil Registration index of births, marriages and deaths for England and Wales, and to provide free Internet access to the transcribed records.

FreeCEN **http://www.freecen.org.uk/cgi/search.pl** Free-to-view UK Census returns online.

GENUKI **http://www.genuki.org.uk** This site offers a collection of genealogical information pages for England, Ireland, Scotland, Wales, the Channel Islands and the Isle of Man.

Our Thanks

**We'd like to thank the following for their contribution
in helping us produce this book:**

Gail Collins

for providing valuable Internet resource links,
and for keeping the spirit of genealogy alive

Juanita Hadwin

for her ongoing help in answering genealogy questions
and for proofreading and checking the manuscript for technical accuracy

and to other friends and family members for kindly making available
some their own precious genealogy photographs and research findings:

Natalie Drache
Grace Camasura
Paul Smith Family
Rebecca Chalmers
Heidi Smith
David and Suzanne Thompson
Diana and Shannon
The French Family
The Taylor Family
The Hoole Family
Pauline and James Simpson

INDEX

NEW
HOLLAND

First published in 2008 by New Holland Publishers (UK) Ltd
London · Cape Town · Sydney · Auckland

Garfield House
86–88 Edgware Road
London, W2 2EA
United Kingdom
www.newhollandpublishers.com

80 McKenzie Street
Cape Town 8001
South Africa

Unit 1, 66 Gibbes Street
Chatswood, NSW 2067
Australia

218 Lake Road
Northcote, Auckland
New Zealand

10 9 8 7 6 5 4 3 2

ISBN 978 1 84773 072 5

Editor: Amy Corbett
Design: AG&G Books
Production: Laurence Poos
Editorial Direction: Rosemary Wilkinson

Photographs were taken by Cheryl Smith herself, were old photographs she had
in her possession or were supplied to her by relatives and friends. All photographs
supplied were prepared/edited for use in the book by Cheryl Smith.

Reproduction by Pica Digital PTE Ltd, Singapore
Printed and bound by Times Offset, Malaysia